MW01708480

LEADERSHIP UNLEASHED

Awaken Your Extraordinary Leadership

Discover how to live and lead
with passion, intention and
unwavering commitment

Pamela J. Griffiths

For permission requests, write to the publisher, addressed
Attention: Permissions Coordinator
info@pampgriffithscoaching.com www.pamgriffithscoaching.com
St. Catharines, ON Canada

Production Editor: Cynthia Lamb

Proofreader: Linda Pruessen

Page Layout: William D. Marler Graphic Design

Cover Design: Don Wininger, Spritz Creative

Cover Photograph: Robert Nowell

Ordering Information: www.pamgriffithscoaching.com

Printed and bound in Canada

ISBN 9-781999-493806

This book is dedicated to my brother Doug.

I wrote this book to help high achieving women around the globe return to themselves. To reinforce what I learned about burn out and how misalignment of my values, passion, purpose and goals caused unnecessary stress. How being caught up in the busyness of life can cause overwhelm, incongruence and erodes our spirit. How mindfulness and authentic alignment brings us back to who we really are, and who we are meant to be.

To choose courage over fear, to shine your light brighter and live a life with passion, freedom and fulfillment.

Acknowledgements

With deepest gratitude.

To my brother Doug, the catalyst in helping me find meaning in my life, who continues to be a source of inspiration. Dan and Meg, this is for you.

To my clients, whose trust and support have made this book possible. Your insights have greatly enhanced these chapters.

To my family, friends, and colleagues who have challenged and inspired me over the years.

To my mentors and coaches who recognized my potential and invested time cultivating it. I am forever grateful.

For my husband, my biggest fan whose belief in me often extends beyond my own. You continue to inspire me in all that you do. I am grateful for your love, patience, and support over the years in helping me make this possible.

For my three beautiful children who inspire me, speak their truth, seek out the best in me, and have shaped me as a parent. Lauren: for your support, patience, your wealth of insight, and inspiration. Thank you for walking with me up to the final hour. Brittany, you cheered me on, held me capable and were a valuable resource when I needed it most. Evan, you challenged me to be a better parent and forever changed who I am today.

For my two step-children, Zac and Tara, who continue to add more layers of love, laughter, and insight to our family. Thank you for enriching my life.

To all of my children: follow your passion, work in your strengths, trust your internal wisdom, continue to raise your bar, and never settle. May your light always shine brightly.

For my parents, whose love always supported and helped me lay a solid foundation, ingraining personal responsibility and a striving to do and be your very best.

For my mother, who trusted in me and gave me a great deal of responsibility and helped shape who I am today.

For my father: my role model and source of inspiration who taught me strong values and the foundation to achieving extraordinary results. Work hard, believe in yourself, and never give up. Helen, your wisdom, encouragement, and support over the years has been invaluable.

To my brother Grant for your willingness to give coaching a try and see what happens. Thank you for your eagle eyes, authentic feedback, your love and confidence in me. Your work amazes me and inspires so many.

To my book coach and editor, Cynthia, for your incredible guidance and helping me develop and complete this final product. Your patience went above and beyond as you continued to hold the integrity of my work. If I only knew then what I know now. Many times when I thought it was "done" it wasn't. Cynthia, your humour helped along the way. She said, "It is done. At least this phase is."

To Bill for your gift to create, intuitively and what appears effortlessly. I'm delighted you played a key role in turning this into the product it is today.

Kate, your brilliance and fresh eyes helped me bring it home.

Don and team for your boundless creativity.

To Christine, Wendy, and Jan who helped me in the initial stages.

To John for putting the spark in me ten years ago.

I am deeply thankful to each of you and grateful for the abundance of love and support in my life. Trusting my internal wisdom to follow the nudges is how this book came to life.

While this is my first book, it's not my own. It belongs to each of you who have touched my life in a big way, those whom I may not have mentioned, and those I have yet to know.

Table of Contents

Introduction

If you were inspired to read this book, you're likely a high achiever who loves learning and developing others. Whether you are a coach, an aspiring coach, a sales leader, or a key decision-maker, you are highly influential (even though you may not know it), and you're here because you're searching for ways to grow beyond your current state. Perhaps you've been feeling anxious, wanting to produce greater results with barely enough time to even meet your current responsibilities. Working through that paradox is often one of the biggest challenges when trying to make a significant change. You may have a deeper sense that there is a better way, and that's why you're here. Throughout these chapters, you will discover that instead of speeding up to get more done, you will be more effective when you slow down, breathe, reflect, and focus. It is in this state where you will feel centred and experience real change.

Perhaps you're here because you are feeling called toward something bigger. Or maybe you had an epiphany like the one I had several years ago while immersed in a graduate-level coach training program. I saw some gaps in the coaching industry, and the first one was actually my own. I had been coaching leaders and teams at the time and realized I did not have a clear process established. My process was intuitive and self-taught. While I was very successful with that approach, and I'm a firm believer in intuition, my process could only take me so far. I had become extremely frustrated with my results and began second-guessing my leadership and coaching ability. I realized that I needed to work on myself in order to lead others more effectively. I also noticed that leaders are lacking vital tools to coach their teams in a more meaningful and powerful way–and some of these tools must come from within.

Whether this book is your first taste of coaching or coaching has been a part of your life for years, you're here now because you want to make a change and are ready to grow. Congratulations for picking up this book and investing in yourself!

If you want to learn more about what coaching can do for you and those you support, you're in the right place. Let me be clear: making change isn't easy. Your effort and commitment to doing the work are part of the process that will move you from your current state to where you want to be. Because your work starts from within, I am inviting you to take a personal journey through these chapters, by completing exercises along the way, so that you can LIVE and LEAD your life with passion, intention, and unwavering commitment! Your reflections will help you dream bigger than you ever have before.

Regardless of where you are on your journey, I'm excited you're here! One thing I know for sure is that none of us are meant to do this alone. When we are trying to achieve something bigger, support is vital to reach the level of impact we want to have.

Note: I use "coach" and "leader" interchangeably throughout my work. I firmly believe that if you want to be an extraordinary leader you need to be a great coach. I often give examples of coaching in organizational settings, but these are also applicable to various other settings such as entrepreneurial and personal life. I encourage you to consider how the essence of these examples can apply to your life and relationships.

Why You Need to Be Here Now

Over the past two decades I've coached entrepreneurs, coaches, and leaders within the corporate world, have been an entrepreneur in my earlier years, and have developed my own successful coaching business. Straddling both the corporate and entrepreneurial arenas has provided me with a unique perspective that I continue to impart in my current business development programs and International Coach Federation (ICF) accredited coaching programs. Over the course of my career, I have been fortunate to work with some of the brightest, inspiring, and talented coaches, leaders, and entrepreneurs. Some oversee multimillion-dollar businesses. Others are committed to building them. Observing them in action as they build confidence and tap into their unique capabilities is a true honour. One similarity that I've noticed amongst them is that they each wear many hats. As their roles and responsibilities increase, the demands on their time become greater than ever before.

While businesses are running with leaner structures and limited resources, we are having to do more with less. Do you find yourself running at high speed with the expectation to produce the same results with fewer resources? The outcome is that we feel more stressed, anxious, and burnt out because we have less time to slow down, breathe, be present, and focus on what's important. Let's face it: it's challenging to manage all of the distractions and competing priorities in today's environment of constant change. Yet, we are still using old methods to try to fix today's problems, and it isn't working.

The next generations are becoming more selective in their job searches, choosing organizations that align with their values, not just their skill sets. Hierarchical systems are losing authority, and we actually need to continue in that direction. We need flatter structures that remove excess layers of middle management, pushing leadership down and encouraging an easier decision-making process. This creates a workforce that is self-motivated, and able to self-manage rather than be managed, and increases levels of self-responsibility and accountability.

These antiquated systems present opportunities to apply our own unique brilliance and reshape organizations. We each bring specific experience and knowledge to the table. We may have read books on how to inspire others: some of us have learned management skills to improve business results, or completed assessments about our emotional intelligence (EI), personal strengths or motivations. We have acquired so much knowledge, –from masters degrees to leadership development to PhD programs to on-the-job training. Yet most of us have not been trained in a true coaching methodology, which can help us learn how to shift the perspectives, beliefs, and thought patterns that have been ingrained in us since childhood. One of the outcomes of learning a coaching methodology is that we learn to shift our *own* thoughts, and through that process we can then help others do the same.

Our behaviours are deeply-rooted, and our default as human beings is to repeat what has been modelled for us. We apply these tendencies in our various roles. If you're a manager, people may come to you with problems, and you become their problem-solver. *You* end up telling them your solution in the hope that they'll get the results you need. This may feel like the most efficient approach so that you can get back to the ever-increasing demands of your role and growing to-do list. After all, your solution has worked for you, so it will work for them, right? Not so much. You will discover in the chapters ahead that this approach is not effective and one size does not fit all. It is unlikely that an employee will be motivated to complete the task exactly your way or attain the results you're hoping for unless you have their buy in.

Here's the good news–you're not alone. A directive approach, or "telling," is a common way most of us engage in conversation and a useful leadership style in specific business operations or in your personal life. I will share with you why this type of transactional leadership style isn't the most effective way to lead and how the shift toward being a transformational leader will help you remain competitive in your industry.

Hope for the Future

Approaching business the way we always have is no longer sustainable. The new speed of change requires different thinking. For instance, it may sound counterintuitive to slow down your thinking, yet this helps you become more purposeful. It speeds up the decision-making process by helping you become more strategic, saving you time in the long run.

In order to produce different results, today's leaders must learn how to do things differently. When we discover our roadblocks and how to observe our own behaviours, we learn how to show up differently. Through this process we can achieve different results.

There are billions of brains around the world being shrunk by outdated communication styles, which is not surprising or anyone's fault in particular. We start our early lives as geniuses. Our minds are like clean slates, wide open to possibility. Over time our childhood experiences, our school systems, and society gradually shrinks our thinking. The very way that we have learned to exchange information (telling versus asking) minimizes our potential and limits what is possible for one another. Fast-forward to our adult lives, where we end up playing small and unintentionally keeping others small. This comes at a cost to ourselves and those we support, including our families. It is how most of us have been raised. We may not be able to solve the bigger systemic issues, such as some antiquated education systems, but we can change how we ourselves lead others.

A quote on the website for the National Aeronautics and Space Administration (NASA) reads: "accomplishments of NASA demonstrate vividly that humans can achieve previously inconceivable feats." NASA certainly has proven this since its inception in 1958. I share this because coaches help clients achieve impossible futures. There is so much untapped potential in our own lives. Just imagine for a moment if you accessed only 2% of that untapped potential. What would be different? We are much more capable than we realize. We all experience self-doubt at one time or another, believing that we're not smart, skilled, or deserving enough; so we fly under the radar and play it safe.

As coaches, we remind our clients of their unique brilliance and capabilities. Coaching is not just about creating outstanding business results (although it does do that too!). Applying a coach approach engages more brains, develops human potential, and helps us think differently. Applying a coach approach as a way of being opens up endless possibilities and can make our world a better place *one conversation at a time.*

If you're thinking, "I don't have time to even think about hiring a coach let alone coach my team" because you're already too busy, I get it. I'm here say that, if you are tired of spinning your wheels, want better results, and feel a deeper calling for something bigger, you *must* find a way to make time. You are worth it. (Yes, I'm telling you!) Carving out time is a prerequisite to making any kind of change in your life. My intention is to help you do this over the next few chapters.

What Coaching Is and Is Not

Before you begin your journey toward playing bigger in your life and having more impact, let me be clear about a couple of important things. Just as graduate or professional degrees are not the be-all and end-all for being a successful leader or business owner, neither is working with a professional coach the only method towards creating positive, lasting change and creating extraordinary results. It may, however, be the most overlooked and undervalued.

On the topic of professional coaches, I don't want to assume that you are fully aware of professional standards, as there are many contrasting views and thousands of credentialed and non-credentialed coaches out there. For the sake of clarity, let's review the definitions I employ throughout this book.

What is coaching? How is it different from mentoring and consulting?

Coaching. The ICF, the gold standard and the world's largest body of professional coaches, defines coaching as "partnering with clients in a thought-provoking and creative process that inspires them to maximize their personal and professional potential." *(coachfederation.org).* Coaching accelerates the client's or team member's progress by providing greater focus and awareness of choice. Through the process of coaching, clients deepen their learning, improve their performance, and enhance their quality of life.

Mentoring. There are many similarities between coaching and mentoring. Mentoring, particularly in its traditional sense, enables an individual to follow in the path of an older and wiser colleague who can pass on knowledge and experience and open doors to otherwise out-of-reach opportunities. Coaching, however, does not require the coach to have direct experience of their client's occupation.

Consulting. Consultants are hired for their knowledge or expertise, often industry specific, and work in an advisory capacity with their clients. Coaches draw out the internal wisdom and capability of their client and help them become self-directed. The coach's role is to ask questions, not to think for the client or solve their problems.

What You Will Learn

In many organizations, coaching skills are simply not part of a leader's tool kit. If they are, the bigger challenge is applying them day to day.

If you are a leader, entrepreneur, coach or aspiring coach, this book can help you discover:

- Your passion
- The art and science behind the skill of asking questions
- Powerful long-term benefits of coaching
- How to become a better listener, coach, and influential leader
- How to shift your leadership style from directive to engaging
- How to empower others and evolve human potential
- Simple, effective ways to motivate, create self-responsibility, and accountability

- Strategies to feel less stressed and more confident
- Your values and the importance of aligning them to your goals
- How to overcome obstacles that keep you stuck
- How to make deep, lasting change
- How to lead from the inside out through the practice of mindfulness
- How to define next steps as you continue your journey toward becoming an extraordinary leader

If you are an aspiring coach this book may ignite your calling. It is therefore important to note that; prospects are becoming more aware of what to look for in a professional coach, and they're doing their homework to ensure they hire qualified candidates. The good news is that the number of credentialed coaches is growing. Professional coaches have attended a rigorous coach training program and have met the standards required by the ICF. Depending on their particular type of training, professional coaches can also provide specific levels of organizational support.

It's time to dive in. As you reflect and authentically record your responses to my questions, I hope you will begin thinking in new ways and expanding your awareness. I'll show you what coaching can offer you and/or your workplace. My hope is that you walk away with powerful tools for both your professional and personal tool belts, discover the very best method to engage others, and have greater impact with those you influence every day.

Grab your favourite pen, find a comfortable chair, and let's get started!

Change is constant. We can choose to change or change will happen to us.

Chapter 1

How to Thrive Today and in Decades to Come

The Great Recession, which began in 2008, was the worst global economic downturn since the 1930s, with the loss of millions of jobs in nearly every sector. Canada's recession was not as brutal but still accounted for the loss of more than 400,000 jobs. While the recession is largely over, its repercussions are still being felt today.

In response to the downturn, organizations decreased their work forces, first by skimming off the fat of their arguably top-heavy management teams. In every industry across the board, the remaining leaders had to produce more results with fewer resources. While this was a reasonable response at the time, like a virus the phenomenon took hold and never let go.

And what happens when all the fat is gone? Well, you start cutting into the main ingredients: the meat, the vegetables, and the broth. Thus, many organizations were left with an underwhelming pot of soup.

So how do organizations continue to do what they've always done? For example, design, produce, market, sell, and deliver one million widgets a year to their customers and clients, when former teams of ten are reduced to teams of five? Team leaders often try to accomplish this by working harder and driving their teams to do the same. When facing a specific deadline this method can work; however, it's not a sustainable long-term practice.

Technology and Its Impact Today

Another factor in our business and personal lives is technology, which has become a blessing and a curse. We simply cannot live without it (or can we?). Computers and smartphones promise to increase our efficiency, saving us time and resources. We have come to rely heavily on these communication tools to retrieve, exchange, and store information in seconds. As a result, we have ramped up our expectations of what we can achieve. Even those of us who remember typewriters take for granted how much more we are now capable of doing in a day. The dichotomy is that instead of feeling we are accomplishing more, we feel as though we never get enough done. The constant distraction of our smartphones impedes our ability to focus and be effective. Our attention is divided when we are expected to always be "on" or available. While technology allows us to do much more with less (including fewer team members), we still cannot manage to keep up. At least that is what we believe to be true.

The eight-hour workday has already become antiquated in many ways. Instead, we're often tuned in evenings and weekends or outside of our work schedule. Many of us struggle with work-life balance and find it increasingly difficult to step away and say, "Today my work is complete. It is time to turn the cell phone off, unplug, and refuel my tank." The seven-day workweek is becoming the new norm, and it's no wonder we are feeling more pressure to keep up.

Being connected to our devices 24/7 comes at a cost. It impacts our ability to be present, takes a toll on our health and relationships, and can eventually lead to burnout, which today's workforce is experiencing in epidemic proportions.

On a scale of 1-10, how would you rate your work-life balance?

(1 means you're not at all happy with the balance of your work and personal life. 10 means you're very happy and work-life balance is perfect for you.)

☐ 1 ☐ 2 ☐ 3 ☐ 4 ☐ 5 ☐ 6 ☐ 7 ☐ 8 ☐ 9 ☐ 10

Part of the solution to creating a sustainable work-life balance is to work smarter, not harder. That sounds simple, but it's not easy to implement. I get it. You might be wondering, "How do I figure out what's not working? And how can I eliminate my list of to do's and stop feeling overwhelmed?"

In the pages ahead, I will cover some of these key considerations as well as important first steps to working smarter, not harder.

Permission to Be Human

Organizations that are transparent and strive to earn your trust provide opportunities for growth and experience far greater business success.

The culture and values of an organization, as well as its opportunities for growth, are as important as compensation and benefits packages, according to the Consumer News Business Channel *(Dickler)* and the Great Place to Work report *(2016)*.

Unfortunately, cultures of high trust are rare. In most organizations, people are afraid to speak out. They are concerned that if they speak openly, they risk being judged by their peers, their manager,–or worse, getting fired.

There is increasing opportunity for leaders and organizations to create workplaces where people trust one another and can be authentic and transparent. While we've all heard the advice about keeping work and home life separate, at the end of the day we are the same person personally and professionally. Being professional in the workplace doesn't mean we need to put on a mask. At work, have you ever felt that you couldn't be who you really are?

While being able to compartmentalize some aspects of home and work is necessary, those threads are woven into the fabric of who we are. We are not meant to be two different people living in one body. We have different roles that we play: mother, father, son, daughter, sister, brother, best friend, confidante, manager, leader, CEO, business owner, peer, coach, mentor, etc. Yet who we are at our core does not change as we move in and out of our roles. Many of us at one time or another have felt the need to be someone other than who we truly are. It is my intention to help you become authentically you.

Having a safe place (and a methodology) at work to broach difficult conversations, where people can express their true selves and share their challenges and opportunities, builds a foundation of high trust amongst employees in any organization, no matter what size. For instance, if you are working 16 hours a day, your marriage is at risk, and you see your children only when you're tucking them in at night, you may be thinking, "I don't want to keep up this pace and don't know who to turn to." Or, if you have just been promoted, and love that you were asked to fill the new role, you might nevertheless be feeling completely out of your league.

Coaching conversations with the right coach can be the perfect mechanism to help us navigate the complex lives we live. These conversations are safe and give us permission to be human. My clients share stories with me that they have never spoken out loud before. Most of us stay in our heads, thinking, thinking, thinking, and never share those thoughts because we don't have a safe place to go.

Who do you turn to when everyone turns to you?

A professionally trained coach is someone you can trust to have your back, be a neutral sounding board, and be skilled at supporting you to work through your current challenges or opportunities.

If you have that person to turn to, great! If not, I recommend finding one. Getting the support you need, where you can be yourself as you navigate change, is often a missing puzzle piece. I have included a link to ICF-certified coaches in the resource section, if you feel ready to move forward and get the support you need.

When we are coached, we hear ourselves express our thoughts and desires out loud for the first time. The more we do this, the more we begin to "self-coach"; that is, to coach ourselves from the inside out. Clients will often share successes and situations where they have self-coached between coaching sessions. Mindfulness is a by-product of coaching: the more coaching we receive, the more aware we become of our thoughts. Another benefit is that when our desires are spoken out loud, they get their first taste of reality. If we take that a step further and write down our thoughts, desires, and goals, they take physical form. You will experience the power of this process in the upcoming chapters.

I'd like to share a story that describes the value of coaching for a client who was in conflict.

After several months of coaching and seeing her thoughts and behaviours from a new perspective, a client had become highly aware of her behaviours and was beginning to self-coach. She came to the realization that she needed her manager to *ask*, not *tell* her what to do. She was feeling that he did not trust her capability and wanted to find a way to raise the issue with him. We discussed how she would tackle the conversation in such a way that he would really hear her. She walked away with my 5-step process and was able to resolve the conflict quickly and get back to a positive working relationship.

If you find yourself needing to have a courageous conversation, here is my 5-step process. It helped my client resolve her conflict, and you can easily adapt it to fit your situation.

5 Steps to a Courageous Conversation

1. Start the conversation and maintain a neutral tone.

"After reflecting upon our last conversation, I realized I reacted abruptly when you told me you wanted me to ______________________________.

2. Take responsibility for your actions or inactions.

"I'm sorry if my reaction offended you. It wasn't my intention to…."

3. Ask for permission to provide feedback and context.

"Is it okay with you if I share why I reacted the way I did?" If the response is yes, say, "When you said ______________________________ (e.g., you have to travel to 16 cities in the next three weeks) I felt __________________ (e.g., I was being micromanaged) and that you __________________________ (e.g., didn't think I was capable of managing my own travel schedule and results)."

"Had you engaged me by asking me what my plan was instead of telling me what to do, I would have been excited to discuss my plan with you and committed to the results."

4. Thank them, remain open and ask for effective feedback.

"Thank you for listening and allowing me to share my feedback. What are you thinking now that you've heard that?" Listen and Explore.

What feedback can you provide me that would enhance my______________." (e.g., communication style and the way we work together).

5. Complete the conversation and commit to next steps.

"How can we move forward effectively?"

It takes courage to coach "up," meaning asking powerful questions and providing feedback to someone you report to. You might feel apprehensive about having this type of conversation. However, when you make a powerful request to have a courageous conversation, it is an opportunity to take your relationship deeper. Providing feedback in a non-judgmental way is a gift to the person you engage with, as most of us are unaware of the impact our actions have and appreciate open, honest feedback. Applying the 5 Steps to a Courageous Conversation can significantly improve your work environment and develop your confidence to lead with intention.

For example, my client's manager was appreciative of the feedback , but at the same time, he had his blinders ripped off. He was completely unaware that he was coming across as a micromanager. He told my client that he was feeling pressure to deliver results and that translated into a modus operandi of overdone strength. That equates to micromanaging. He realized why she was frustrated and wanted her to own her results. This client had built a long-standing relationship with her manager, and through coaching she developed the courage to make a powerful request in order to thrive in her role. She knew the stakes were high but was willing to risk it rather than stifle her voice and keep her manager in the dark. It was a humbling experience for him and an empowering one for her, and it brought their relationship to a new level of trust.

Coaching conversations grant you permission to be human.

Coaching Conversations Are Cost-Effective and Change Lives

If you are concerned that coaching conversations might feel "airy fairy" and require more of your time, you are right! Initially they do. If you're worried that work won't get done or that your bottom line will suffer, I understand your concerns. However, whether you're a CEO or a team of one, consider the costs of not working with a coach. As I shared earlier, your investment in coaching frees up time for activities such as working on key initiatives and connecting with staff to get a pulse on how they're doing. Working with a coach helps us to be more strategic, get out of our own head, and build confidence and momentum to reach our goals.

Before I continue, let me be clear: I am not suggesting that everyone in your organization or on your team should receive one-on-one coaching from an external coach. That wouldn't be sustainable and is too cost prohibitive for organizations. If you have the resources and are inspired to do that, you are at an advantage and will see results more quickly. However, if one-on-one coaching is not easily accessible to you, group coaching programs are a cost-effective option that can be equally as effective in achieving your goals. For larger organizations, it is more cost-effective to train internal coaches, building internal bench strength that supports employees over the long-term.

5 ways that coaching conversations can impact your bottom line and your life.

1) **Fewer sick days.** The cost of burnout to organizations through sick days or LOAs (leaves of absence) is huge. Studies suggest that burnout (including stress, overtime, workers compensation, productivity and excessive turnover) contributes to an estimated loss of $300 billion across US businesses *(Leiter & Maslach 3).*

   Because coaching helps us listen more deeply, mindfulness is a by-product of coaching. Mindfulness is being aware of and present with our own thoughts, without judgement. Mindful living practices enhance our well-being and the well-being of those we support *(Niemiec & Lissing).* When leaders are taught coaching skills, they are better equipped to support their employees in finding their passion and work-life balance. As a result, coaching not only enhances employee morale, but also delivers invaluable benefits to organizations, including fewer sick days. Therefore, there is a cost associated with *not* investing in coaching.

2) **Increased effectiveness.** When we are tired, and trying to burn the candle at both ends, our brain gets foggy and we are not as effective.

   Do you find yourself repeatedly distracted? Do you waste time reading insignificant emails, being pulled off task, and then working well past your regular hours to do the work that must get done? If so, you're not alone. We all get distracted; it's normal. Coaching conversations help us step away from our day-to-day distractions and look at ways to be more effective and stay laser-focused on our goals.

3) **Slowing down to speed up.** Another powerful benefit of coaching is that coaching conversations actually slow our thinking down, which results in speeding things up. We can toss and turn ideas in our minds for days–even years. The time we waste spinning these thoughts in our head is unproductive. This idea of slowing down to speed things up may sound odd but consider this: Do you run at high speed all the time? Do you find yourself wishing and hoping you had more money, a new job, new home, new boss, new career, a husband or wife, over and over again?

   When we share these thoughts, ideas, challenges, or opportunities with our coach, all of a sudden the idea becomes real. Now that we have said it out loud, we can do something with it. Whether you let it go, brainstorm, overcome, achieve, or just notice it, addressing your ideas allows you to move forward.

   If, for example, a sales team wants to increase sales but is busy each day dealing with internal conflict and administrative tasks, leaving them limited time to focus on key activities, their desired results are likely minimal. If, however, the team had a leader who helped them identify their challenges and tap into their motivations, how might that impact their results? Through getting coached by their leader, the team would discover how to maximize their time and focus on key activities, such as sales calls to increase results.

4) **Authenticity breeds confidence.** When we walk around wearing masks because we lack the confidence to stand up for what we want and show up as who we really are, there is a cost. For example, if you were asked to dress in traditional corporate attire and work behind a desk each day, when you feel your best in casual business attire, interacting with people out of the office (or vice versa), how would that impact the way you show up each day? You might feel stifled, distracted, and out of sync, which can impact your energy and confidence.

   The truth is, when we are asked to do something that does not align with who we are, we can feel like an impostor. We automatically get more traction when we feel congruent and can be authentic in roles that align with our unique abilities. When we are doing great work and feel aligned, authenticity shines through, which helps us connect with others easily. We naturally feel more confident as we live happier, more productive lives. Coaching conversations help us know our strengths, align our values and be true to who we are, which makes us feel more energized. When we are more energized, we experience greater results, and the ROI (return on investment) becomes evident.

5) **More courage.** In *Lean In*, Sheryl Sandberg talks about a time when she hosted a meeting. The few women who were there sat around the boardroom watching the men talk. They didn't even want to join them at the table. They sat back observing, not leaning in and making their voices heard*(27)*.

   Too many women are afraid to speak up, and those who do worry about the repercussions they may face. Coaching helps us have courage, find our voice and resolve any conflicts that may arise as a result. If you were to bring more courage to your work–personal life, what would be different?

   I have experienced this myself by being very open and transparent and having said things in boardrooms that were perceived as a little too outspoken (for a female). I have even been pulled aside by what I then assumed to be well-intentioned (female) peers who told me that I should keep my mouth shut and be an observer if I want to keep my job. I felt like a child being reprimanded. Those statements or values did not align with mine. Can you relate?

Over the years I have observed leaders who shut down their teams' ideas by being overbearing or controlling and not empowering others to share their thoughts on how to move things forward. As you will see in a moment, this behaviour doesn't cultivate creativity, innovation and capability–it stifles it. As I said before, leading this way is not anybody's fault–it's how many of us were raised, and we often don't realize how our behaviour impacts others.

Whether we are a spouse, daughter, caretaker, manager or CEO, our voice matters. We all have strengths, values and a unique lens that can contribute to the greater good. Coaching conversations help us have a voice, step out of our comfort zone and be more courageous. In addition, coaching increases ROI by providing the space to think more strategically, enhance well-being and ultimately be more effective.

Reflection

What courageous action can you take that would make the greatest difference? ____________________

____

If that action then became a daily ritual, what impact would it have in your career/organization/life a year from now? ____________________

____

Shrinking Thinking

Consider this: How did you get to where you are today? In our lives and careers there have been people along the way who helped us grow. Many of us had caring parents and caregivers who raised us and helped us take our first few steps. Some of our parents, teachers, mentors, siblings, friends and colleagues encouraged us, and without them, we would not be who we are today. Through each of them, we observed, we learned, we listened and we evolved. None of us stayed the same: to some degree or another we grew. We are human and we were created to grow. When we are not growing we begin to shrink, and when we shrink we feel small. We are all capable of so much more, but most of us choose to play safe. This is in part due to the stories we have told ourselves and have carried forward to our current reality.

Marianne Williamson said it best: "Our deepest fear is not that we are inadequate. Our deepest fear is that we are powerful beyond measure... Your playing small doesn't serve the world. There is nothing enlightened about shrinking so that other people won't feel insecure around you...And as we let our own light shine, we unconsciously give other people permission to do the same" *(190-91)*.

Reflection

What would you do if you were not afraid? ____________________

How would that impact your life? ____________________

Think back to when you were young. Were you told what to do? Most of us were, to varying degrees. Few of us were ever asked what and how we wanted to do something.

We must foster relationships that empower us, create positive outcomes and help us to thrive. It's time to reverse the shrinking thinking that began years ago. In his TED Talk, Sir Ken Robinson described how young people lose their ability to think in "divergent or nonlinear ways" *(Robinson 2006).* Divergent thinking is the process of exploring many possible solutions to a problem; it's "thinking outside the box" and is a key component of creativity. This is compared to convergent thinking, which is utilized in a multiple-choice test, where you focus on a limited set of options and choose the best among them. Obviously, difficult problems require divergent thinking and it is "essential for the new economic circumstances of the 21st century" *(Robinson 2010).*

This critical ability, however, was trained out of most of us.

Many of us hold the assumption that we start our lives lacking intelligence and need education to acquire it, which we do over time. However, as you'll see, that is untrue–at least in the traditional sense. In fact:

1. **We all have the capacity for creative (or divergent) thought.**
2. **Our ability to think creatively deteriorates over time.**

In his TED Talk, Robinson shares a study that measured the divergent thinking of 1,600 children aged 3 to 5 and found that 98% could think in divergent ways. By the time they were 8 to 10 years old, 32% could think divergently. When the same test was retaken at ages 13 to 15, only 10% could think in this way. When the test was given to 200,000 25-year-olds, only 2% could think divergently *(2010).* Imagine where we would be today if we were able to think in more unique and expansive ways!

This shrinking thinking is not happening naturally. Robinson lays some of the blame on the education system, which is too often driven by the idea that "there is only one right answer and it's at the back of the book." This stifles creative thought. It also happens because we educate children in batches by their birthdates and tell them "this" is what you have to learn and here is how you do "it". Because this is how many of us were taught, it's the way we tend to teach others, and it's also why it's innate for us to tell people what to do.

Most schools do not tap into creativity, treat students as individuals, or acknowledge that we do not all learn the same way. Instead, most education systems only measure a few kinds of intelligence, while in reality there are 8 or 9 different kinds, each representing different ways of processing information *(Gardner)*.

Teachers are expected to deliver curriculum in a condensed time frame and ensure that the students achieve great marks. That's a lot of pressure for both teachers and students, given the complexity in classrooms today. What often ends up happening is the children do not fully understand the material. Teachers don't have time to thoroughly check how their students are doing because they're busy delivering curriculum, marking, and supporting students of all learning styles and levels. Being a teacher today is much more complex than ever before. I have heard and seen firsthand how challenged, stressed, and burnt out some teachers are. Who could keep up? If you're a teacher, you might be thinking that slowing down on any given day to customize an approach is a great concept, but putting it into action is challenging, to say the least. I concur, but I know it's possible.

Corporate sales trainers face similar issues when teaching sales leaders how to improve results. Trainers have to deliver the training in a limited time frame with the expectation of increased ROI. There is a big push toward delivering high-quality content to train sales teams, and yet not enough time to check in and see if the trainees are understanding how to apply what they have learned. I have been a corporate trainer responsible for business growth and leadership development, and I understand that in this role you're accountable to increase sales each quarter. Management's agenda is that the sales leaders learn the content (regardless of their learning style or knowledge of sales), and when the training is complete, they are expected to start selling with confidence. (And hurry up–we need to triple sales this month!) The expectation is that after training, the sales leaders should be up to speed with the knowledge required to do the work. The fact is, the majority are not. The highest-scoring trainees under the most skilled trainers will still only increase their effectiveness from 1 or 2 to 5 on a scale of 1 to 10, while the rest of the trainees will lag far behind. In fact, a study of 31 public-sector managers found that training *alone* increased productivity by 22.4%, but the addition of follow-up coaching to the training increased productivity *(Olivero et al. 466)*. This compelling study reveals that choosing not to invest in coaching could be costing you valuable resources on various levels.

If we don't slow down to ask questions, and instead simply tell people what to do and how to do it, we shrink their thinking and limit their potential to achieve what they are capable of in their own way. When we couple coaching and training, we help individuals anchor their learning and attain better results over time.

It's Time to Shift from Telling to Asking

The heart of extraordinary leadership is to learn how to ask questions of those we lead and of ourselves. This is also how we can begin to not just stop shrinking thinking, but expand the minds of those we lead. As I mentioned, much of the time we default to problem solving, taking on the responsibility to resolve problems rather than holding others capable of finding their own solution. As you become more skilled at asking questions, you ultimately open up more time in your day and, therefore, begin to work smarter, not harder. This happens because those you work with will begin to self-coach, a by-product of coaching, and attempt to find their own answers rather than come to you for them.

Here's an example of shrinking thinking occurring in a workplace setting:

> **Employee:** "I'm really struggling to figure out how to do X, Y, Z, and I'm feeling a lot of pressure because it has to be done by Thursday."
>
> **Manager:** "Okay, all you need to do is…(manager trying to solve the problem)….Now you have everything you need to know. I expect outstanding results by (insert impossible deadline here)."

That may be a little exaggerated, but it's not atypical of many day-to-day interactions at the office or home. While the directive approach may feel like the fastest, most efficient way to approach a situation so you can get back to your own pressing deadlines, it will cost more time in the long run. This approach may be necessary in some situations (such as emergencies, when someone needs specific advice, or when someone requires technical training), but it's not the best way to get the most out of others. When our teams, peers, or children are not thriving, we tend to lay blame without considering there might be something fundamentally wrong with our approach.

What are the risks of applying a directive approach day-in and day-out?

- It doesn't help people grow, create awareness, or change behaviours.
- It doesn't invite them to step into their full potential or consider a new way forward.
- We significantly reduce our chances of creating "buy in"; meaning, to convince others to believe in and commit to a cause, vision or goal.
- People are less motivated to do what needs to be done.
- We shrink people's thinking.
- We make an enormous number of assumptions when we tell and don't ask.
- People may lose morale and feel undervalued.

And the list goes on...

Shifting from telling to asking empowers individuals to take on more of the decision-making and become self-responsible. This method pushes leadership down and ensures we are growing rather than keeping people small and under our command.

With that said, I'm proposing we learn this coach approach to encourage the people we work with to find their own solutions.

Here's how to accomplish this:

- Ask questions to stimulate thought rather than stifle it.
- Share our stories to provide insight and then turn that insight back to them to see what fits (if anything).
- Stay open to what others think, as we don't know if our way will work for them.

Applying this approach helps us to motivate others and support them to do their own thinking, eventually creating new pathways in *their* brain.

Insight Comes from Within

There's another compelling reason to using a coach approach instead of a directive approach: for insights to be useful, they need to be generated from within. This is true for several reasons, as made evident by David Rock and Jeffrey Schwartz's research.

First, when people have an "aha!" moment they experience an adrenaline-like rush, creating their own insights and making new connections in the brain. We experience this rush like a positive burst of energy. This may be key to facilitating change, as it overrides internal and external obstacles, such as the stories we tell ourselves or those "Negative Nellies" that distract us from making big change. However, the "aha!" moment is just the beginning. To make big change, this process needs to be repeated over time to become embedded in our mind, affect our behaviours, and create new habits. As when we learned how to drive a car or quitting smoking, we need to be supported to be successful so that we don't revert back to our old ways.

Second, our neural pathways are influenced by our genes, experiences and what we pay attention to. We have general functions in common, but we each have our own unique brain composition. Our brains are so complex and individual that it would be a waste of time to try to tell someone else how to think in an attempt to reorganize their thought patterns. It is far more effective and efficient to help others come to their own insights and become aware of their actions. To accomplish this, we must ask questions and practise being the observer of our thoughts and behaviours. In his 1759 masterpiece, Adam Smith referred to this as being "the spectators of our own behaviour" *(Gocmen 60)*.

Third, what we pay attention to on a day-to-day basis influences our very being. "The term "attention density" is increasingly used to define the amount of attention paid to a particular mental experience over a specific time. The greater the concentration on a specific idea or mental experience, the higher the attention density. What we focus on grows. When we pay attention to particular experiences or ideas they become an intrinsic part of who we are, how we perceive the world, and how our brain works. This is another reason why coaching works–it helps us to keep our goals front and centre.

You may have had the experience of attending a new training program, feeling excited to learn and experience new ways of thinking, but later realizing that you can't remember what those new ways of thinking were. Did you like what you learned? Or maybe you weren't able to pay attention long enough to fully get it? Did you notice that something was missing from the experience?

What is often missing is the use of a coach approach as a mechanism to engage participants and integrate material in bite sizes, which helps to solidify the learning.

Finally, the human brain can behave like a 2-year-old: if you tell it what to do, its automatic default is to push back. This is partly because the brain naturally tries to maintain a stable environment and avoid change. It also happens because the brain has an innate desire to create its own new connections. In other words, it doesn't like to be told what to do. It wants to experience for itself. What's the alternative? Scientific evidence suggests that asking powerful questions changes the brain *(Rock & Schwartz 6)*. This is the art and science of extraordinary leadership. Asking rather than telling needs to become a best practice so that our clients/teams/peers/children not only find their own solutions, but also become self-directed and create new pathways in the brain. This can create powerful and sustainable change by transforming who we are and how we see the world. When we change the brain we ultimately impact our future generations.

Professionally trained coaches are skilled at asking questions that engage the prefrontal cortex of the brain, the area responsible for problem-solving and decision-making. When we do this, we help our clients create new neural pathways. Repeated over time, this approach has proven to help create lasting change.

Creating Thinking Cultures

Shifting to a coach approach also increases employee engagement. With decades of experience researching hundreds of organizations and millions of employees, Gallup is the world leader in understanding engagement and its impact in the workplace. According to the Gallup Q12 questionnaire, only 30% of employees are engaged. That means a whopping 70% are not reaching their full potential. When you think about how this connects to the bottom line, the finding is significant. Unsurprisingly, Gallup suggests that disengagement is negatively impacting the economy. There's a direct correlation between engagement and productivity across diverse sectors around the globe *(7)*.

Engagement can be negatively impacted by using a directive approach. When we tell others, "We have to increase numbers, hurry up, make it happen, and here's what I want you to do," we get push back. We light up their amygdala (the fight, flight or freeze part of the brain), and they become disengaged. If we've told them to accomplish a goal our way, and it's not how they would do it, or they need more time to think of a different approach and we're rushing them to the finish line, we risk shutting down their motivation and creativity. We take away their power to resolve the challenge themselves. As a result, fewer will reach the goal that's been set.

On the other hand, when we empower others to think for themselves and find their own solutions, we help them see their contribution; they feel valued, respected, appreciated and challenged–in short, engaged.

Attract and Retain Top Talent

(How to keep the intellectual property from leaving the building)

Leaders and employees alike are becoming more and more aware that a directive approach isn't working and are feeling that they want to be developed. If they're not being challenged in their organization, the best and the brightest will leave the building for those organizations that do adopt a coach approach and focus on developing talent.

Another unfortunate shift has taken place over the past decade, as companies have downsized: there are fewer and fewer resources being invested in training and leadership development. Leaders are thirsty for growth. We need to learn, be challenged, and step out of our comfort zones.

Companies that empower their people, tap into their creativity and help them see what's possible are the companies that will lead the way in the future. They will attract and retain top talent, which, of course, will positively impact the bottom line.

Change is constant. We can choose to change or change will happen to us.

Using a coach approach helps us manage and thrive in change. It also creates thinking cultures and develops leaders who give their best to those they lead, who, in turn, give their best to them.

My physical space–where I live, play and work–is beautiful too.
Life is barren without it–beauty inspires and renews the soul.

Chapter 2

The Beauty of Transformation

In this chapter, I share the story of how I found my life's work. As I do so, I'll be drawing attention to the common threads that have woven throughout my life and career: following my inner compass, an entrepreneurial mindset, and building confidence in others to do extraordinary things through coaching. My path is my own, yet many of the milestones, turning points, and key realizations are likely similar to ones you've experienced. I think it's worth drawing attention to these commonalities. We are all unique, and yet, in very important ways, our respective journeys mirror each other's.

Born to Be an Entrepreneur

I started my first business when I was 12 years old. I would spend summers at my family's cottage turning plain, wire coat hangers into handcrafted closet décor. I could barely keep up with the orders. Of course, wire coat hangers wrapped in Phentex aren't exactly all the rage today, but at the time I was excited by my creative skill and sales ability. The point is, I was a tween who and had not yet been exposed to what the world had in store for me career-wise, (outside of helping my mother care for my baby brother and helping my father on weekends in his printing business). However, this experience revealed something integral about me; I've always been drawn to transforming the plain into the beautiful. The coat hangers sparked a trend that has woven its way into everything I have done in my life. I love to be surrounded by beautiful things in my environment, my home, and my business. Are you aware of a common thread or interest from childhood that runs through your life?

Throughout high school, like many girls, I was drawn to fashion. My older sister was studying cosmetology. I thought I might follow in her footsteps, since many of my friends were constantly asking me to style their hair or apply their makeup. It seemed I had a natural flare for it, so I became their go-to image consultant for social events long before I had any formal training. I noticed early on that my makeovers had a direct impact on how people felt, adding a spring to their step and a smile to their faces. Knowing that I was able to influence others in that way was rewarding. Plus, it came easily to me, and it was fun. This is an important part of knowing your own strengths: if it comes easily, it's an innate gift. And the best part? It doesn't feel like work!

When the time came, I attended a vocational school that offered cosmetology as an option. Choosing a skills trade enabled students to work in their trade once they graduated. Cosmetology opened the door to learning, and provided opportunities to work in the field of esthetics and hairdressing. In addition to enjoying my studies, I felt this was the fastest path to accomplishing my goal, which was to finish school with a career and make money. I had zero desire for higher learning based on the options available at the time. My parents weren't exactly impressed when I told them my plan. I think they had a different one in mind for me. Looking back, it seems my path was right for me at the time, and I was fortunate to know what I wanted early on. I was out earning a great income while many of my friends in college were floundering, trying to figure out their next step. It's not easy for young people to figure out what to do with the rest of their lives.

During my days as a stylist, colour technician, and cosmetic artist, I was passionate about helping women look and feel good. I loved hearing how their new look made them feel and watching their confidence soar. I did well as a stylist. I started at the bottom and slowly worked my way up, building a loyal clientele while developing my skills and knowledge. Years later I was recruited to join a new team in a larger, more progressive salon that offered greater earning potential. That was my next stepping-stone, and the timing was perfect. I was ready for something bigger.

It's true what they say about hairdressers and their clients. My clients told me very personal stories. Week in and week out they updated me about their lives. I listened and shared my thoughts. While I wasn't a coach at that time (coaching wasn't even in my realm of thinking), it was here where I learned the value of listening and being present. Little did I know I was laying the foundation for my future.

I loved my new environment. The team travelled to the latest and greatest hair conventions to learn and stay on top of trends. After several years of success, something began to shift. My dream had been to open a spa where women could come to relax and be pampered. I had wanted to create a safe place for women to de-stress so that they could walk away feeling renewed, re-energized, balanced, and ready to tackle their challenges and opportunities. But somewhere along the line, my dream changed; I no longer wanted to open the spa. I wanted to have a bigger impact in a different way.

After reinventing myself several times throughout my career, I now know, that we humans don't stay the same (thankfully). My cosmetology career took me eight years down one path before my dream began to shift. This shift stemmed from an internal feeling that things were no longer lining up. It was a call toward something bigger and, like many of us, that call wasn't clear to me at first. I felt unfulfilled, my energy was low, and I had lost my passion. I wasn't being challenged and felt as if I was shrinking. The work no longer aligned with my values. It was time to move on. I knew I needed more; I just wasn't sure exactly what that was, and I didn't know who to turn to.

Have you ever experienced that feeling of being off-kilter, stagnant, or stale? You may no longer be excited to get up and go to work in the morning, and you finally realize it's time for something else. That's normal. We're human and we continue to evolve, one thing eventually leading to another, from the time we are conceived until the end of our life. We change. We learn. We grow. It's a cycle.

It's not surprising to me that millennials will change careers 8 to 10 times in their lifetime, and four times in their twenties alone. This is the new normal.

The catalyst for me came when my best friend's father, who was like a father to me, passed away. The following week I gave my two weeks notice without knowing what I was going to do next. I just knew that after eight years, I had to leave the field. I had a small reserve of savings to carry me for a few months, and a lot of faith that things would work out. I didn't see a bigger career path in the industry other than opening my own business. After a period of reflection and time spent listening to my inner wisdom, plus feedback from a few close friends and family, that's what I did–only it looked a little different from what I had originally envisioned.

Reflection

Have you ever taken a big leap of faith, knowing you had to trust your instinct? ____________________

____

What was it? ____________________

____

What prompted you to do it? ____________________

____

What was important about taking action? ____________________

____

What changed as a result? ____________________

____

What did you learn? ____________________

____

____

Did your learning help you understand your motivations the next time you were faced with a big decision? I imagine it did, and that experience has immeasurable value.

A leap of faith can feel freeing, exhilarating, and scary all at the same time.

It's important to listen to our instinct, take risks, and stay open to possibilities.

Playing Bigger

I was drawn to understanding fashion and beauty not just as something women need in order to appeal to a potential partner, but instead as an authentic way to open the door to our own power. I found an outlet to satisfy this interest in image consulting. I had heard about and researched a global direct sales image company, a competitor to Mary Kay, that was expanding into Canada. The concept excited me. I would have my image consulting business under their umbrella. I could help them expand into a new territory, help women look and feel good from head to toe, and conduct image workshops for corporations, all while remaining my own boss and connecting with women entrepreneurs across North America.

The business would incorporate much of what I already knew, and I would be well paid for sales and developing my team. Direct sales organizations are known for their unlimited earning potential, offering a career ladder without the corporate glass ceiling. I was hooked; I'd found my people! There was only one hitch. I had to move out of province, as the company didn't have a license to operate in Montreal, QC, where I was born and raised. Moving to a different province was a big leap for me. I didn't know a soul other than my dad and his wife. I didn't have any contacts other than a few people they knew. Still, I took the leap and made the move. People close to me thought I was nuts for leaving (a consistent theme in my life. Can you relate). I was motivated, however, and knew I was on the right path with a lot to learn.

In order to become one of their certified consultants, the company required that we attend a rigorous training, which covered everything from how to run a successful business to skin care, colour analysis, cosmetic application, body typing, and how to conduct consultations and group presentations. I gained a new understanding of what hot, warm, and cold leads meant, and how to prospect, interview, book, sell, and recruit over the phone and face-to-face. I started my business from scratch, in a new territory, with no clients. I began to build a team, training and coaching them to do what I did. Whether I was scheduling image makeovers or conducting group presentations, I was having fun! My clients wanted to learn more about their image, how to dress, and how to preserve their skin while they were still young.

When I moved to my new province, I was not entirely on my own. The company provided a fabulous mentor who knew the business inside and out. She had a natural gift for developing women. In her words, she would "move in" with her aspiring leaders. At the time, it was easy for me to get distracted by thoughts that sidetracked me from my goals. For example: Maybe I'll count my inventory instead of picking up the phone to speak to clients. She knew my goals and saw my potential and called me weekly (sometimes daily) to make sure I stayed on track. She instilled the value of consistently taking big action every day that would have a direct impact on my bottom line. She taught me the importance of focusing on business-building activities rather than on busywork like filing, laundry, or tidying up my home office (a potential risk for new business owners working from home). Over time, I learned systems to support my success.

Biannual leadership conferences were open to all business women. Those who were serious about learning and growing attended in droves. The focus of these events was to train business leaders and inspire women to do more than they thought possible. We were taught how to sell, recruit, build a team, and train our teams, which I had started doing right away (knowing relatively little about it). Sometimes jumping in with two feet is the best way to learn and embed a new skill so that it becomes second nature. The more you do the better you get, with a little feedback and, of course, support!

You've heard the saying "ignorance is bliss," meaning, what you don't know won't bother you. Sometimes it's better not to overthink things. Taking a leap can be the best way to learn!

Reflection

Can you think of a time when you wanted to learn to do something well and you simply jumped in and started doing it without a great deal of preparation or study? ____________________

____

What happened as a result? ____________________

____

What did you learn? ____________________

____

I was in my element, except when I had to push my growing edges (opportunities for growth), but I learned to feel the fear and do it anyway. I continued to grow my client base, increase my income, earn cars, trips, jewellery, and more. I rose through the leadership ranks and consistently earned awards in sales, recruiting, and leadership development. Nevertheless, it was a big surprise to me when my mentor said, "You know, you're in the top 5% of leaders in this company." (Not surprisingly, so was she.)

She would say, “The pace of the leader is the pace of the pack.” I was just doing what I knew was required to succeed. I felt normal, not extraordinary (although my thoughts tried to tell me I wasn’t successful enough).

My mentor was key to my success. Why? Because she cared. She had walked the path that I was on, and I was able to learn from her mistakes and successes. She knew the business inside and out. Prior to signing on with the company, I had been very intentional, asking to be connected to one of their top leaders. I knew instinctively that I needed a mentor and someone to hold my feet to the fire. This experience exposed me to the value of a mentoring/coaching relationship.

My time in the direct sales business was an eye-opening experience, filled with travel, friendships, and an amazing lifestyle. I soaked in top-notch training and did what I was trained to do, assessed what worked and what didn’t, found support, and experienced tremendous personal growth.

I loved my work. My clients wanted to learn how to improve their image, and my team members wanted to know how to grow their business, and be more confident and successful. My clients left with their spirits lifted and my team would leave our meetings or coaching sessions feeling inspired, ready to tackle new challenges and increase business results. I was in my element.

Today, the “Avon calling” stereotype may seem rather antiquated; however, direct sales is currently one of the best industries for women to learn, grow, and thrive in (more than 95% of the people in direct sales are women). These organizations are all about coaching women to reach higher levels of success and experience personal growth through training and leadership development. It’s a portal that attracts a diverse range of women, from those who want to earn extra income without sacrificing too much time away from their families, to teachers, accountants, doctors, and lawyers who are drawn by the unlimited learning potential. Women are not told what they can’t do; instead they are nurtured, mentored, and trained to do and be the best they can.

In fact, direct sales is the oldest form of selling, dating back to fur traders in North America. Since Avon’s inception in 1868, and especially since the 1950s, when the company’s door-to-door business model boomed, the industry has liberated hundreds of thousands of women around the globe, providing an acceptable avenue for women to work at a time when women weren't "supposed" to be employed.

Direct sales organizations give women the opportunity to stretch and grow themselves, their income, and their leadership potential. It was in this space where I experienced tremendous growth, mastered the art of business, and discovered my passion for coaching.

Beauty remains one of my core values, though my understanding of what it truly means has changed and deepened. When we believe in ourselves, love who we are, and honour our values, we carry ourselves differently. We stand straighter and we reflect our positive thoughts and self-worth through our facial expressions and body language. This is how we express our beauty from the inside out.

When I'm coaching others, I'm "in the zone" and I see the beauty within, not by pretending that everyone is beautiful, but because there truly is beauty within everyone.

My physical space–where I live, play, and work–is beautiful too. Life is barren without it–beauty inspires and renews the soul.

Clarifying Your Passion and Purpose

Reflection

What are your core values? ______________________________

____

What are some of the common threads that have brought you to where you are today? ______________________________

____

Sales 101–Taking a Coach Approach

(The following applies to all sales professionals, regardless of whether you are a coach or a sales leader.)

Running my own business taught me a great deal about sales. Presentations and lunch-and-learns provided opportunities to get referrals and potential clients. I learned how to market and build my prospect list, engage in sales conversations, qualify leads, and turn those leads into sales, referrals, and new team members.

Sales is like coaching; it starts with a conversation. You set out to learn by asking questions about what the potential client or team member's goal is, what they're struggling with, and what they're ready for. Sales is a process that takes time and evolves from one conversation to the next before a potential client decides to buy. It may take longer to close the sale depending on what you're selling.

There are many factors involved in that decision-making. You gain clients (or customers) when they come to know, like, and trust you. Part of what I teach today is a coach approach to sales; learning how to ask questions and listen for the client's readiness to move forward. Selling isn't about being pushy, yet that's how many of us perceive it, so we may shy away. The challenge is, shying away from selling doesn't help people. Selling is simply a conversation in which you listen for how your product or service fills the client's need, if at all. If it does, but they're not ready to move forward, your job is to stay in touch. As I learned and taught my team, these leads go into your sales funnel and eventually come out the other end when they become your clients or customers.

Like many people, I learn by doing. You've heard the expression "feel the fear and do it anyway." That's how I became comfortable asking for the sale. I started with one-on-one consultations, then upgraded to small groups and eventually to large audiences. Learning to get comfortable with being uncomfortable is the way to conquer our fear of change; we grow by getting uncomfortable. Presenting to thousands of people is exciting, and I have

come to recognize the power in overcoming your fear. It is truly a privilege, and it's a way to influence in a bigger way.

I was the shy one in high school, who tried anything to get out of presenting in front of the class.

Thirty years later, main stage is a comfortable place for me to be.

I encouraged my team to face their fears as we expanded the company's presence in the eastern region. I trained them to sell and recruit, coaching them to move up the leadership ladder, all the while continuing to grow my own business.

With each expansion came the opportunity for me to overcome my own fears as well. In fact, fear was my biggest challenge, and yet it's what continues to fuel my success in business. "What if I fail?" "What if they say no?" "What if I don't know what the hell I'm doing?" "How will I ever be successful at this?" Coaching has given me tools for dealing with those intrusive voices, not only for myself, but also for those I work with. Marj Busse refers to these thoughts as "quacking ducks," and I'm aware when they show up. I may feel trapped for a moment, but then I am able to push them aside and realize they are just thoughts.

Helpful for understanding thoughts and awareness is the work of Eckhart Tolle, who teaches us to simply observe our thoughts and then let them go. I love this idea of separating mind and thought. In *A New Earth*, Tolle writes, "Awakening is a shift in consciousness in which thinking and awareness are separate…instead of being lost in your thinking, when you are awake you recognize yourself as the awareness behind it"*(259)*. This is powerful! This helps us simply observe our thoughts rather than buy into them and allow them to have power over us–especially the thoughts that try to keep us small. This awareness is the path toward becoming an extraordinary leader–and also great at sales. If we're second-guessing ourselves, our clients won't believe in us either.

Whether these are completely new ideas that feel a little "out there" or concepts you're familiar with, you may find reading Tolle's *A New Earth* helpful in building greater awareness.

Reflection

What thoughts get in your way as you move toward your goals? Write them down. For now, just notice them. ______________________________

____

When are they likely to emerge? ______________________________

____

____

When you read them now on paper, are these thoughts real or perceived? In other words, are they valid or something you've created in your mind that's not necessarily true? ______________________________

____

____

In *Wishes Fulfilled: Mastering the Art of Manifesting,* Dr. Wayne Dyer teaches a technique for retraining your subconscious mind so that you stop believing in your negative thoughts. He advises flipping these thoughts into positive ones; for example, "I am not successful" becomes "I am successful."

Let's practise this now. Turn your negative thoughts into positive, affirming statements; for example, " I am successful, wealthy, smart, deserving, loving, happy, healthy, fit," etc.

I am... ____

____

____

____

____

Own these thoughts and envision yourself already happy, healthy, successful, etc.

Let them be your mantras.

As Dwyer also said, "What you focus on grows."

If the negative thoughts persist, remember they are only thoughts. Noticing this helps to defuse their power. Thoughts come and go.

Post your positive thoughts (mantras) where you can see them every day. Repeat these affirmations daily.

Baby Gap and Going Corporate

After several exhilarating years in direct sales, it was time to graduate again. The company's leadership changed and their new direction did not align with my values. After 10+ years in the field I was ready for something bigger, and I could feel the discontent internally. I wanted to venture into the corporate world, and this idea had been percolating for a while.

As you transition through your life, it's important to listen to your authentic inner voice and not allow others' opinions to get in the way of what you really want.

Observe and be aware of those who may try to limit your success. People close to me, including my ex-husband, said, "Why would they hire you? You don't have experience. You'll never get a leadership role at that level." I would say to myself, "Oh yeah? Just watch me!" It wasn't the first or last time that negative feedback from others has fuelled my will to succeed.

Their negative feedback might be their own ducks quacking, the very ones that keep them stuck. Or maybe they didn't know me as well as they thought, because hearing "it will never happen" made me even more determined to make it happen! And I did, but not right away. I was several months pregnant at the time with my third child and that became my priority and focus.

Learning to trust your instinct is a process, and just like a muscle, instinct needs to be exercised.

The kind of corporate coaching and training role I was looking for wasn't easy to find; it was like searching for a needle in a haystack and would entail substantial travel. One day, while walking down a city street after an interview, I looked down to see my protruding belly. It suddenly occurred to me, something was wrong with this picture. I noticed my inner voice whispering to me, "Go home and focus on this baby now. Come back when the timing is right." I was reminded of my priority and focus in that moment.

You might be thinking, "Gee, Pam, that wasn't exactly rocket science! You were 7 months pregnant!" But when we are filled with anxiety, trying to make ends meet, or focused on a task or idea, it can be difficult to still our thoughts and think things through rationally. I followed my inner voice. I had to trust that we would make ends meet, and somehow we did. I took a break for a year and a half, so my career has a little "baby gap." Although it was difficult to put my dream on hold, I knew at a deeper level that this was the right decision. I aligned my choices with what was important to me. As women who bear children, raise families, and have careers, we can feel torn between maintaining our independence–our earning potential and fulfilling all the roles that we play: mother, wife, daughter, friend, aunt, sister. Alignment of your values (whatever they are) is key. This wasn't an easy time for me. While I love my children and watching them grow–they inspire me in so many ways–I also love making a difference in the world with my work. I've learned to not feel guilty about that, because doing great work actually makes me a better mom, wife, friend, etc. It fulfills me and rounds me out.

Reflection

It's important to have goals and to pursue them diligently. And it's even more important to be in alignment with those goals.

Have you ever been so focused on achieving something that you overlooked what's important in your life? The values that make you who you are?

What did that feel like? ____

____

What steps did you take to come back to your centre? ______________

____

____

In 2001, when my third child was 18 months old, I was ready to return to my goal. I was recruited for a corporate role with a global, Australia-based skin care/cosmetics and nutritional products company. This was the natural next step for me. I transferred my field training, development skills, and knowledge to this new role, on a much broader scale.

I loved the learning curve and seeing the business from the production side of the fence. This widened my lens to operations, systems and integration, event planning and execution, sales and marketing, KPIs (key performance indicators), budgets, and deliverables. At the time, I reported to a successful CEO who transformed my thinking, particularly during one quarterly sales manager meeting that I will never forget (nor will my former colleagues, I'm hunching.)

It was just before Christmas and we arrived at the office early, as usual. (We always had fun together–we worked hard and played hard, too.) After we finished our other meetings, the CEO joined us about mid-morning and gave us our new mission, which was to recruit 1,000 new consultants in the month of February. We were speechless. (I actually think our jaws dropped.) Growing that number of new recruits, especially during the shortest month of the year, seemed impossible. Oh, and one more small detail: this news was delivered a week before Christmas! We all thought we would finish our workweek and fly home to prepare for the holidays with family. But our CEO had other plans for us.

She spoke about the need to change our paradigms, to which I remember thinking, *Hmmm, this is a new concept… and, what's wrong with our paradigm?* While I was grappling with that idea, she helped us experience exactly what it meant to change our paradigm. Up to that time, the company had grown slowly, and the maximum number of new recruits brought into the business in any given month was 200. We knew we had to grow faster but couldn't imagine this quantum leap. Clearly, we needed a new paradigm.

With determination, perseverance and a *big* shift in thinking, we surprised ourselves and reached our goal. In fact, we exceeded our numbers. We rallied our troops and trusted each other to make it happen. This was the greatest gift and my biggest takeaway at this stage in my career. We reset our expectations of what was possible, developed a plan, and then helped our field leaders see the possibility and empowered them to make it happen. When we can bust through our own thinking, we can help others bust through theirs.

Two years later, the company started eliminating the top-level leadership roles and, as a new hire, I was among the first to be let go. Additionally, my marriage was falling apart. It was scary, unknown territory, and all happening at the same time.

While I knew I was part of a minimum 2-year mandate, losing my position still came as a shock (the writing was on the wall, just not large enough for me to see it). I was worried; "How will I make ends meet? What if I don't find another role like this one? Roles like this are rare and hard to find. Who will hire me?" Those were the stories I told myself, and they were pretty loud!

Despite my worries, I decided to take the summer off and just be. Enjoy some downtime and play in my garden. I had been longing to spend time outside enjoying the weather and my wish came true (although not in the way I had imagined!). I needed time to decompress from my formerly rigorous schedule. My other takeaway was that I needed to redevelop healthier work habits, which I had lost. I had become increasingly focused in my work, and there never seemed to be enough time in the day to refuel my tank. We started early and finished late. Often I would have dinner with the kids, hang out for a while, and then slide back into my office often until late in the evening. That's the way it had become, and I knew I needed to get back to firmer work boundaries in my next role.

A few months later, I received a call from a former colleague who was working with a global company that had an opening for a similar role. It was another gift, a natural next step with another extraordinary opportunity. A few weeks later, I started my new role with this large, direct sales organization, which produced digital and paper scrapbooking supplies. This was a big shift from the beauty industry. I was responsible for business growth, specifically increasing sales and growing leadership. I was in my element, developing their "shining stars," grooming new leaders, and helping the organization think outside the box. I learned so much from my colleagues and gained a reputation for being one who consistently challenged existing processes, pushed the envelope, and broadened thinking. I reminded people of their brilliance and helped them step into their potential.

I also developed and delivered training and key leadership messages at our national conferences and field meetings across the country. I coached leaders and teams, identified target markets, and contributed to sales and marketing plans. Working with the senior leadership team, quarterly reviews and strategic planning exposed me to many facets of the business that had experienced tremendous growth over the years. With over 90,000 consultants around the globe we were doing all the right things (or so we thought). It was an exhilarating time in my career. I loved my role, the team, and the company.

The Turning Point

After my divorce, however, some tough years ensued. Being a career-oriented mother with three children under 10 was challenging. Thank goodness for my two nannies, Brenda and Arlene (identical twins), whom I sponsored from the Philippines. For the record, arriving at this decision wasn't an easy process. I needed to reframe many of my assumptions and beliefs, such as asking for help, second-guessing my ability to cover their salaries, and trusting someone I don't know with my children.

These women have the biggest hearts, and I'm so grateful to have them in my life. They were like my right arm. I couldn't have done what I did without them. I trusted them with my children and, when I had to travel, I knew my kids were safe. Hiring them was one of the biggest and best decisions I ever made. Moving from their home in the Philippines, they made sacrifices many have never had to make. They took risks and paved the way for their families to have a better life. Their courage makes me smile. It fills my heart knowing I played a small part in helping them fulfill their dreams. They started a new life here, bought their first home, and have brought their husbands and children to join them. They went back to school, have found new careers, and continue to grow and thrive today. They are trailblazers, leading the way for other women.

I want to stress here that you don't need to recreate what was modelled to you (what your mother or father did) if it's not working for you. You don't have to be a product of your experience. Society and cultural norms can put a lot of pressure on how we live and the choices we make. An example: the idea that you're not a good parent if you're not running all day, every day and night, driving your children to and from school and multiple sports activities. Many of us struggle trying to conform to these norms. We seek approval by living in these self-limiting square boxes with unwritten rules only to find out that it feels inauthentic and exhausting and is not sustainable. You get to choose what's right for you.

Reflection

What social or cultural norms have you noticed yourself conforming to that no longer fit? ____

____

What trail would you like to blaze? ____________________________

____

____

What do you need to let go of in order to make that happen? _______

____

____

In 2006, everything shifted for me again. My younger brother, who was diabetic, died at the age of 34. He left behind two beautiful young children, ages 3 and 7. I had sensed that he wasn't long for this world. Yet, of course, when it actually happened, I was shocked and devastated.

He used to visit me with his children almost every weekend. One particular day he told me he would be attending a Christmas party the coming weekend and wouldn't be coming over. All was fine until I received a call from the mother of his children. She had expected him to pick them up, but he hadn't. When I heard this, I assumed he had neglected to tell her about his plans–which turned out to be untrue. An alarm went off in my mind. I called him immediately.

When he answered his phone he was slurring his words. I assumed he was at a bar and that he had been drinking. I felt a surge of annoyance and began to question him: "Where are you? Have you eaten? Are you driving?" He replied, "I'm at the bar across the street from my apartment. Yes, I had a bite, and don't worry, my car is at home." I was so frustrated! Didn't he realize that with diabetes he shouldn't be drinking, for God's sake? He reminded me he had a Christmas party to attend the following evening and wouldn't be home with his children that weekend, which I had forgotten. I said goodbye.

My questions were legitimate and some of my assumptions were accurate, but I was frustrated and was asking from a place of judgment. I wasn't fully present. I was distracted, caught up in my own perceptions, and wasn't treating this conversation as if it could be our last. He passed away later that evening.

We found out later that his blood sugar levels had been really high. Not knowing my brother was diabetic, the bartender had served him sweet shooters all night. That wasn't the bartender's fault. My brother was very social; he was full of life and loved having fun. That night he had ordered rounds for himself and his friends. That was the last night they saw him.

In the aftermath of my brother's passing, I have reflected on our last conversation often. Rather than being angry with him, I could have asked him to please pass the phone to someone near him. Not knowing if his blood sugar was high or low, I could have urged him to eat something, which may or may not have helped level it out. I felt guilty at first. I should have known; he'd had other diabetic health emergencies in my presence. I knew that when a diabetic's blood sugar is low (or high), they may slur their words, even sound or appear drunk. But that night, I was so caught up in my own frustrations that I didn't fully process what might be going on. In other words, I didn't take time in that moment to cut through the noise, both external (what I was hearing from others) and internal (what was going on in my own head), to listen more deeply to what was happening underneath the surface. This experience reminds me to slow down and treat every conversation as if it were my last.

There is no guarantee, of course, that my brother would have survived, but if I'd been fully present–not just to his words, but what was behind the words–perhaps I could have intervened one more time. I'll never know, and it's not my fault.

My brother's death had a huge impact on my life. In fact, it's my reason for writing this book. I remember one day, shortly after his death, I was drawn to a picture of him on my desk. In that moment, I started to question if I was truly in the right place, and whether I was doing what I needed to be doing. This was another turning point in my life.

Though my journey in the corporate world had been a magnificent opportunity and possibly the greatest learning I'd experienced to date, I no longer felt in control of my life. For a while, my role had been shifting, and I was doing less of what really fuelled me. I had lost my passion; the travel was becoming too much and I needed more time with my children. I was no longer willing to pay the price for the life I was living. I yearned for peace and tranquility.

Eventually, I realized that I had to pinpoint what was truly important to me. I needed to realign my values and reconnect with my roots. Given the shock of my brother's death and the turmoil the company I was working for became embroiled in, it took me a couple of years to truly clarify what I wanted.

Reflection

Unexpected things can cause big shifts in our lives. My brother's death was the catalyst that caused me to sit up and notice that I was no longer living a life that aligned with my values. It was time to re-evaluate what was important.

Can you recall a time when something unexpected moved you to re-evaluate your life? ______________________________

____

What did you learn from that experience? ______________________________

____

____

Just over a year after my brother died, and just before the recession took hold, the company I was working for filed Chapter 11. Still in the fog of processing my brother's death, I could only put one foot in front of the other. This is not uncommon when you have experienced an unexpected loss or tragedy. Abruptly, I was thrown into a world of ambiguity. What did this mean for all of our jobs? Who would be let go first? What would happen to our families, clients, and income?

The uncertainty dragged on for years. Upper management informed us that it was going to be a gradual process and that the Canadian team would be all right, since we were already very lean. Still, we saw the axe come down on hundreds of U.S. employees, and there were constant rumours swirling around of our imminent demise. Were we ever going to stabilize and regain momentum, or would we just keep shrinking?

The field leaders were scared, embarrassed, and losing faith in the company. I could not figure out how to encourage them to persevere. We all felt as though we were in a downward spiral. I felt stuck. Forever changed by my brother's death and the questions it raised for me, I simply didn't have any more tools in my coaching toolbox to help my leaders focus on what they *could* control. I realized that I needed a way to revitalize them and to encourage them to trust that we could turn this big ship around.

Blazing New Trails

I received my solution when my dear friend Jo-Ann urged me to speak to a woman she'd met at a human resource conference. The woman was Marj Busse, (whom I mentioned earlier), a faculty member at Royal Roads University. Two months later I was enrolled in their Leadership and Management graduate studies program, while remaining in my corporate role. I had no idea what I was in for, nor did I fully understand the time commitment required for both career and school work, but I was already two feet in!

Attending this program gave me the gift of time to take a good hard look at who I was and who I wanted to be. How often do we get the opportunity to step back far enough to reflect? Doing so helped me recognize the next step I needed to take. This came at the perfect time, and my instinct told me it was worth taking the leap. This journey was transformational and reaffirmed my love for coaching! Only now I was very aware that I needed to do more of it and bring coaching out to the world in a much bigger way.

I thought I knew how to coach. I had intuitively developed my own coaching process and had experienced years of success developing others before I hit a roadblock. Throughout my career, I had attended multiple leadership development workshops and one-day coaching programs, none of which stuck out as transformational learning. It was only when I attended this rigorous coaching program that I became entrenched in the true meaning of coaching. That gave me a deeper understanding of the concepts, behaviours, and skills required to be a great coach. I had intuitively known there is a beginning, middle, and end to a coaching conversation, and now I had learned a conceptual framework to support this understanding. It also confirmed for me that if you lead people–whether you are an entrepreneur or part of an organization–coaching skills are an important tool. The kind of coaching I am referring to isn't just a run-of-the-mill training program. Unless you seek out an accredited coaching program through ICF, such as Royal Roads or a course like my The Coach Approach System™, you may not properly learn core coaching skills or gain a deeper understanding of your true self.

With my newly acquired coaching tools, I ran a six-month pilot program with a target group of leaders. The outcome was extraordinary. Leaders had new hope; many reported tripling sales and told me they were selling more than they ever thought possible. Recruiting increased and they were promoting new leaders in a fraction of the normal time frame (from 4 months instead of the 2-year average). There was focus, momentum, and positivity.

Despite this success, the reality was that the company was in Chapter 11. We soon met for our quarterly meeting, and before I could speak, the general manager told me my position had been eliminated.

I was surprised but not devastated. I had prepared an exit strategy with the help of my coach and my intent had been to give my notice that day. Instead, they picked the date, which in hindsight was perfect timing. It was the summer of 2010. I had just graduated from the executive coaching program and now had the gift of time to start building my coaching business. This was a huge opportunity to bring my new learning to the world.

Of course, I was not completely overjoyed; there were plenty of emotions that accompanied this transition. I was worried and had a little fear. Here I was, a divorced mom with three young children, a mortgage, and all that comes with the territory, transitioning from a full-time career in an established leadership role into the unpredictability of self-employment. I was losing my identity and income! (At least that's what my thoughts were telling me.) I had developed a plan but questioned my capability, even though I had been down this road before. Would I be successful? If so, how? What if…? Can you relate?

I was well aware that the questioning and second-guessing was to be expected. Whenever we are moving through change, it sets off those "quacking" ducks. "You're not smart enough! "QUACK!" You don't know what the hell you're doing!" QUACK! And the negative talk from others crept in, "Who are you to open a coaching practice?" There was a lot of unwanted noise going on in my head. And yet, I also had come to know and trust through each transition in my life that I always land on my feet.

Once in a while our quacking ducks are worth paying attention to. It does not serve us just to repress all of our uneasy feelings. In fact, sometimes what we're hearing isn't a duck at all. It's our inner voice alerting us that something isn't quite right. Maybe we need to have a courageous conversation with someone, or make a huge life change, or end a relationship. Maybe the inner whisper is a nudge to start the project we've put off for too long, explore a new career, or begin a new relationship.

If we fail to pay attention at the right times to that little whisper inside, the situation will often persist until something beyond our control causes change in our lives. This change can feel frustrating or unsettling because it is unexpected and we didn't initiate it ourselves. Sometimes we feel the change happened to us, and we blame the external force rather than recognizing our role in it. We ignore the quiet whisper until it gets too loud to deny.

This is what happened with me. After my brother passed away I knew intuitively I needed a change; however, it took a long time to figure out exactly what I wanted to change. Chapter 11 brought that whisper into the forefront and I made my move.

Reflection

Do your quacking ducks distract you and fuel your self-doubt? _____

____

Do you notice when your inner voice is trying to guide you? If so, how do you distinguish between the two? ________________

____

____

What does this negative self-talk try to convince you of? ________

____

____

Can you think of a time when you ignored your inner voice (your truth) or gut feeling? What happened? ______________________________

____

Is there a time when you've acted on the guidance of your inner voice?

____

____

What did you learn from this experience? ______________________

____

____

Ever Evolving, Yet Common Threads Remain

As long as we're alive, we're changing–evolving and shedding old skin. In my coaching practice, I stress the importance of bringing our actions into alignment with our inner compass. When we listen to our inner voice, it becomes more clear to us what changes we need to make in order to grow beyond our current state. That fine-tuning never stops. It's a continual creative process and that's a good thing, because if we're not growing, what's the point? Resting on our laurels can become monotonous and lead us to feel as though we're not making a difference. While some may live their lives with complacency at times, humans have an innate need to grow. We're here to make a difference in the lives of others and leave the world a better place.

Yet, in a very real sense, I'm still doing the work I started as a young woman. The common thread is clear. In my twenties, I helped women build confidence by improving their appearance. Today I help my clients increase their confidence and go after what they want.

That's our job as coaches: to empower others to stretch and grow. I love helping people live and lead extraordinary lives.

Reflection

Imagine your impossible future, the one you want but think you couldn't possibly have, What would it look like? ______________________

____

____

Life has many surprises in store for all of us. Part of the fun is discovering that, the more we learn, the less we know.

Fast Forward to Today

It has taken years to identify the common threads that are woven throughout my career. When I first started my coaching practice those threads weren't clear. In fact, most of what I was doing was unclear. I had never sold coaching and didn't have a clue how to do it. At first, I struggled for years to get more clients and increase my income. I needed to learn how to market myself and get my message out there. In my next phase of growth, I had to learn how to stop feeling overwhelmed as I was building a thriving business and learn how to leverage myself in order to have more impact without burning out. I've invested tens of thousands of dollars along the way to learn all of this and more. Today I run a successful global coaching and training company. I help coaches and leaders like you live and lead with passion, by learning the essential skills and systems to leverage your time, and increase your impact and your income, while having fun along the way!

Leading from the inside out is at the heart of extraordinary leadership.

Chapter 3

Overcome Your Limiting Beliefs and Play a Bigger Game

Extraordinary leadership is a process that begins from the inside. In order to lead others, we must first learn how to lead ourselves. Similarly, in order to guide others through their own transformations, we need to understand in a deeper sense how to transform ourselves.

Before we dive deeper into this concept, I'm inviting you to experience for yourself what it means to lead from the inside out. This chapter includes a guide that will help you gain clarity about your goals and become more aware of what stands in the way of attaining them. This powerful tool was designed to help you overcome limiting beliefs and develop greater confidence so that you can move forward in a big way.

To reach your goals and achieve far more than you may currently think possible requires thinking in new ways and embracing change. Part of the transformation process involves moving beyond self-limiting doubts and fears as you courageously commit to your bold vision.

Change is the essence of life.

While the process of change is not always easy, it's worth the effort if you want to live a life filled with passion, purpose, and intention.

When we embark on a journey of personal change we inspire others around us. And as we grow and thrive, we also inspire others to do the same.

If you've picked up this book, you're likely tired of the status quo and ready for something more. I'm so happy you're here because I am the expansion queen. I stretch people to reach higher and play bigger! I will guide you through the same process that I've taken hundreds of clients through to help them achieve amazing results. My clients have learned strategies proven to increase performance. Some have built businesses from the ground up, tripled sales, taken courageous action to leave jobs that were burning them out, found work they love, experienced less stress, or developed more confidence in who they are.

I encourage you to take your time as you work through this chapter. Don't rush. Find a quiet place to read the questions. Give yourself time to reflect as you record your responses. Stillness and time are a necessary part of the process to help you tap into your internal wisdom and evoke what's next for you.

The value here comes not from my questions but rather from the heightened awareness they evoke, coupled with your willingness to look inside yourself to seek your truth and examine your mindset. Throughout this process you will gain clarity and confidence to play a bigger game in your life and create an opening for what's possible. It's in you, waiting.

Seek Your Truth–Observe Your Story

Leading from the inside out means that, you are the author of your life and your reason for being. What is the contribution you want to make in your life/career/business?

To be able to make that contribution, you must first become aware of the false stories you are telling yourself right now.

We all have stories in our heads that run like tapes: the stories we tell ourselves over and over about who we are (and aren't), what we can (and can't) do, what we are (and aren't) capable of. Our stories define us and what we believe to be true. These stories come from our parents, teachers, society, and a multitude of experiences. They inform how we perceive the world. They become part of who we are and, over time, become etched into our belief system, whether or not they are real or simply perceived. Rarely, if ever, do we take time to check out these assumptions and listen for our truth.

The point is, even if we are remotely aware of them (and especially if we aren't aware of them!), our thoughts (the stories we tell ourselves) can rule our lives and keep us small. That is, until we become keenly aware of them, and start to choose how we listen and what we do with them.

The first step is to notice and then observe your thoughts. A daily meditation process is helpful for this.

Mini Meditation and Observation Exercise

For this exercise, find a place where you can sit quietly for about two minutes to simply focus on your breathing. As you notice your mind drifting away, bring it back to your breath and focus there. Breathe in and out slowly and calmly.

How did it go? If this was your first time, congratulations! You just experienced a mini mediation practice. Did you find yourself distracted by your thoughts–maybe, your to-do list, or wondering "why am I even doing this?" Maybe you were distracted by noises around you. You may have found it hard to stay focused on your breath. That's normal, but with practice you will get better.

Now ask yourself the following questions. (If you're not used to reflecting on your thoughts, this may be challenging, so just do your best. The goal is not perfection but to become more aware.)

What are the stories you tell yourself? (These are the stories that have led to limiting beliefs–for example, money doesn't grow on trees; leaving my job is too risky; they won't possibly choose me; I will never be a successful entrepreneur.) ______________________________

____

____

____

How do these stories show up in your life? (i.e., I don't have enough money to invest in professional development.) ______________________________

____

____

____

____

What is the real truth? (free of stories, perceptions, beliefs) __________

____

____

If the story you tell yourself did not distract you from your goals, what would be different? ___________________________________

____

____

____

What limiting beliefs are no longer serving you? _______________

____

____

What stories are you ready to let go of? ______________________

____

____

Do you remember some of the stories I told myself when I was in a demanding corporate role and raising three young children? I loved my job at the time. I had to take myself through this process to become aware of the stories I was telling myself. They were keeping me stuck. I then had to take intentional action, creating new pathways in my brain to support positive change. Our stories are often unconscious, and it may take time to pull them into our awareness and bring about change. If you are struggling to identify the stories that keep you stuck, be patient, give yourself space, and get curious.

One particular client I led through this process had moved from a highly technical role to a senior role, managing a large team. While the promotion was a natural next step, there was basically no on-boarding process to help him close the gaps in his leadership. He jumped into the deep end with a new title and office. Ideally, organizations have an on-boarding process to help new managers set a solid foundation, and clearly understand their role, responsibilities, and the expectations within the organization's culture. A good process typically involves a plan for the first 90 days, which sets the new hire up for success, as well as supporting top-level leaders with a coach. In my opinion, all levels need support from a coach during transition.

In the absence of that, my client struggled as he attempted to figure out his role as a new manager. Our coaching conversations supported him in recognizing how much he already knew, which reinforced his confidence in his ability to lead. Through coaching he learned how to lead from the inside out and trust in his capability. His next level of development as a new manager was learning how to lead by empowering his team. He needed to move away from being the "problem-solver," a learned behaviour that has become part of his belief system, to delegating and leading his team.

Making Change

Here is the dichotomy: Everybody wants change and yet, we fear it. Change means uncertainty, and we are biologically hard-wired to fear the unknown. Regardless of our race, we humans like to be comfortable. Change requires being uncomfortable and doing the work. This is why so many people stay stuck and resist the changes they most need to make.

When you think about changing your life, taking a new approach, or venturing out in a new direction, it's normal to feel stressed, anxious, overwhelmed and/or excited. It's natural to experience many different emotions at once. The question is, which thoughts do you allow to guide you?

Feel the fear and do it anyway!

The caterpillar becoming a butterfly is a beautiful example of transformation. Not only does the butterfly look completely different than the caterpillar it once was, but its very cells have changed. The butterfly is a wonderful metaphor for our own ability transform miraculously as we move into different phases of life. We shed the old layers that no longer fit, and emerge with a new set of wings.

As Steve Jobs said, "I didn't see it then, but it turned out that getting fired from Apple was the best thing that could have ever happened to me.

The heaviness of being successful was replaced by the lightness of being a beginner again, less sure about everything. It freed me to enter one of the most creative periods of my life" *(2005).*

Can you relate? I can. This quote perfectly captures what many of us experienced after being downsized.

Reflection

Think of a time when you were forced into change, (e.g., a job loss, divorce, death of a loved one). What did you learn from that experience?

____
____
____
____

What change would you like to make in your life/career/business right now? ____
____
____

When you think of making that change, how do you feel? Happy? Anxious? Exhilarated? Scared? Take a moment to sit with this question. Write down the thoughts and feelings that arise. Be specific. _________
____
____
____
____

How much of what you are feeling is based on fear or limiting beliefs?

____
____
____
____

What will help you move beyond your fear? ________________________
____

Again, take time to allow the question to process if it's not clear for you

____

____

____

"The only way to do great work is to love what you do. If you haven't found it yet, keep looking. Don't settle." – Steve Jobs

Challenging the Impossible

As leaders we often set the bar too low. We need to create bigger goals, take risks, and be more courageous! We can do the impossible. We simply need to shift our mindset and raise our bar. A CEO I reported to years ago exemplified this beautifully during a fourth-quarter regional sales meeting, when she announced her plan for our time together.

I began this story in chapter 2. Here's the ending. It was shortly before Christmas, when we had our sights set on home. Instead, we hunkered down in the boardroom for three days, during which time our CEO expected us to emerge with a plan to recruit 1,000 consultants in the month of February. She left us with the task of figuring out a big, bold plan right after telling us we needed to change our paradigm. She was right–we did need to change our paradigm–but how? Rather than give us the answer, she empowered us to figure it out.

The process was painful: we resisted, we pushed back…we were stuck. We were afraid we couldn't succeed. Our brains hurt. We pulled our hair out trying to develop a plan in only three days to reach a seemingly impossible goal. Frustrated, because it had never been done before in this company, we thought, How on earth can we do this?

We succeeded. We were a lean but mighty team. We came out of that boardroom three days later with a game plan to engage our field leaders and rally the troops like never before. It wasn't easy. We had to be patient. Our leaders went through the same process of disbelief and resistance to change that we had. We continued to promote our vision of a compelling future until, *ta-da!* Our leaders were on board and we accomplished our goal. In fact, we surpassed our goal of 1,000 consultants in the shortest month of the year, more than tripling our results from previous years.

Now, the process wasn't perfect, and we learned a lot along the way. Still, we succeeded. We accomplished the so-called impossible future. And YOU can too!

That experience taught me:

- The impact a leader can have (good, bad, or indifferent)
- The value of support–our CEO believed in us
- To never be afraid to do the impossible
- That when you change your mindset, you can change your life

Reflection

When have you overcome a personal limitation? What did you learn?

____

____

____

____

How have you inspired others to overcome their own personal limitations? ____

____

____

What happened? ____

____

____

____

Have there been times when you approached a challenge with a scarcity mindset (i.e., limited thinking)? __________________________

____

____

What happened as a result? ______________________________

____

____

____

When you expand your limiting beliefs and think bigger, how does it help you? ____

____

____

What is possible in that moment? ______________________________

____

____

____

How does your experience help others? ______________________________

____

____

____

Reframing Your Story

Let's take another look at the thoughts that run through your mind.

It's not easy to revise them. It takes awareness and intention to redirect your thoughts into positive self-talk to ensure you're aligning with your true beliefs, values, and goals.

Revising my thoughts and story took a lot of effort and time (I still haven't arrived). Choosing to let go of the thoughts that try to distract you and stepping away from the everyday minutiae to refocus your mind isn't easy. It's an ongoing journey, a lifetime process of revision, focus, and being intentional.

During a conference I attended a few years ago, a speaker showed us a graphic of a Leonardo da Vinci manuscript that illustrated his creative process. Most of us know da Vinci for his famous painting, the *Mona Lisa*. He was an artist, a musician, writer, architect, scientist, musician, and mathematician. Obviously a creative, successful, intelligent soul.

When the image appeared on the screen, I remember initially feeling shocked that an artist of such fame could be so messy! His work looked so disorganized. I came to understand that out of that disorganized mess, beautifully sculpted pieces of art can emerge. And, for the first time, I felt validated as I witnessed a process so close to my own. I realized that I wasn't disorganized–my numerous computer and sticky notes that finally landed in a binder as organized work was simply my process–my path to producing this book. From brain dumping to refining, reworking, tweaking, sculpting until voila! The final product was unveiled.

I have changed my mindset from "my work is disorganized" to, "this is my creative process." Now I am so grateful that my creative process supports thousands of coaches and leaders around the globe. Wow! It is so freeing to embrace my creativity!

Discovering your own strengths and celebrating others' is at the heart of extraordinary leadership.

Time to Reframe Your Story

Reflection

What old limiting belief needs to be reframed? ____________________

____

____

____

What are your unique gifts/strengths? Which ones are you down-playing?

____

____

____

What is your new mantra? (Positive, energizing story?) ______________

____

____

____

____

Create Your Big, Bold, Courageous Vision

"He who loves practice without theory is like the sailor who boards ship without a rudder and compass and never knows where he may cast."
– Leonardo da Vinci

It is necessary, then, to have a clear, compelling vision and a solid plan to bring it to fruition.

Your vision must align with who you are (your strengths and values) and what you really want.

It's time to dive in, draw your new road map, and plan the best route to arrive at your destination.

Who inspires you and why? ______________________________

What kind of legacy would you like to leave? ______________________________

If you could make one statement that would be heard around the globe, what would it be? ______________________________

What opportunities are in front of you? ______________________________

What is your BIG vision? The one that is so BIG you may not have yet dared to speak it out loud? It's burning inside of you, and you know it needs to be realized. ______________________________

Is this vision big enough? (Have you raised your bar or are you playing too small?) ______________________________

What is important about realizing your BIG vision? ______________________________

How will your vision make a difference in the world? ______________________________

What obstacles or limiting beliefs will you need to overcome to make your vision a reality? ____

____

____

____

What goals are you COMMITTING to? ____

____

____

____

What time frame would you like to achieve your goal by? ____________

____

____

____

Who can support you?

This is key as you work toward your BIG vision. Many people think they can do it alone. It has been my experience that support is critical to overcoming limiting beliefs and growing beyond your current state. ________________

____

____

____

"The journey of a thousand miles
begins with a single step." – Lao Tzu

What is the first step you will take? ____

____

____

____

____

Congratulations for taking the time to clarify your goals! You have taken a big step. Let's take a moment to step back and take a breath. That was a lot to think about.

What does it feel like to put this on paper? ______________________________
____
____
____

"Your playing small doesn't serve the world." – Marianne Williamson

The Paradox of Fear

When you imagined a bigger vision for yourself, did you feel fear? If so, good! Because if you didn't, your goal isn't big enough! We all have fear. It's inescapable. Yes, it can be paralyzing. It can hold us back from being our best self. It can be a dangerous enemy.

You must (FTF and DIA)! That's because taking action cures fear. Inaction keeps us stuck and further fuels our fear. Also, courage is not the absence of fear. Courage is the will to move forward in the face of fear. When we stay in fear, we procrastinate, we become complacent, and our lives don't change.

Now, let's reframe fear for a moment. What if you thought of fear as a necessary evil, or an emotion that has a purpose? The amygdala kicks in to protect us when we most need it. Those "danger, danger" warning signs and spikes of adrenaline ensure that we steady ourselves while hiking up a steep mountain so that we don't slip and fall. Fear heightens our senses and we become more acutely aware of our surroundings.

Fear also pushes our boundaries. It calls us forth to step into our courage, and when we do this, we grow. The more we step up and face our fear, the more confidence we gain. The more confidence we gain, the easier it is to overcome our fear.

Great insights are gained when we arrive on the other side of fear, when we realize that what scared us wasn't so bad after all. Overcoming fear provides us with new clarity and strength. We realize that most of our fears were simply made up, and we ruminated over them for so long that we began to believe them. Once we learn this, we can step back from our thoughts to see that our fear does not define us.

You hold the key to unlock your fear.

You may have heard the parable that if a frog is dropped into boiling water it will jump out, but if dropped in cold water that is slowly brought to a boil, it will not recognize the danger and will meet its end. The frog doesn't sense the changing temperature and becomes complacent to its environment. Like this frog, we too have an internal device that is geared to sense sudden changes, not slow, gradual ones *(Senge 22-23)*. It's the frog's lack of fear about its slowly changing environment that keeps him in hot water.

The slowly rising temperature of the water is also a great metaphor for time slipping by in a relatively comfortable yet fundamentally unfulfilled life. As days go by and we don't take action toward our dreams, we can become stuck in a rut. The habit of staying safe becomes our norm because it's easy. Sometimes a little edge of fear is needed to remove ourselves from a situation that is no longer serving us!

Stepping into your courage and facing your fear is not for the faint of heart (e.g., leaving a steady job to become an entrepreneur, applying for a new role with a large portfolio, being promoted, or leaving an abusive spouse). Fear and uncertainty are simply part of the territory when faced with something new. You may feel uncertain of what your path forward looks like. Your vision may be so big it overwhelms you and you don't know where to start. You may second-guess your ability to succeed. This can be especially true when you have experienced great success in the past and then transition to a new role or phase in your life or business. The stakes feel higher, so the transition can feel scary.

Let's return to your vision and break through some of your fear and discover how fear can serve you.

Reflection

When you think about your BIG vision, what scares you? ____________

____

____

____

What's the worst that could happen? ______________________________

____

____

What is the best possible outcome? ______________________________

____

____

____

Fear can be positive if you know how to direct it. When you feel afraid, remember that fear is part of the great adventure of life. It means your senses are alive. Fear is not your enemy. Overcoming it opens the door to possibility.

Stay focused on your goal and what matters most, regardless of what negative thoughts try to distract you about what "might" happen. Just notice them. Redirect those thoughts and focus on the present moment. Remember, you are resourceful. You have what you need inside you to fulfill your dream. I recommend posting your vision and goals where you will see them every day.

Remember to celebrate the milestones along the way.

Chapter 4

The Impact of Coaching

Our job as leaders is to evolve human capacity. With the speed of change in today's world, this is not optional. If you are struggling to motivate those you support and tap into their innate strengths, then you cannot expect the best from them. One of the outcomes of effective coaching is to unleash the full potential of those you support. Doing so will in turn improve your bottom line. As we've discussed, leaders who utilize a coach approach have far greater success than those who don't. This is why it is critical that coaching skills become an essential leadership competency for all leaders (and we're all leaders), whether one aspires to become a professional coach or not.

One of the core skills of using a coach approach is emotional intelligence, a term that became widely known through Daniel Goleman's bestselling book of the same name. Emotional intelligence is the ability to have heightened awareness of the emotions of self and others. EI, the emotional equivalent to IQ, is as important as academic or technical knowledge and is one of the greatest indicators of leadership success. EI impacts several areas, including your ability to develop your own personal leadership and your ability to develop others. When leaders have high EI, they understand the effect they have on others. They are self-motivated, more aware of the motivations of others, skillfully manage relationships, and create positive, productive workplaces *(Wilcox)*. Particularly at the top levels in organizations, where technical skills are much less significant, emotional intelligence is key.

We are beyond the days of the "carrot and stick" approach. By this I mean the practice of offering incentives for hitting a target. If the target isn't hit, there is no cash bonus, or all-inclusive trip to the Bahamas, or promotion up the career ladder. This type of "reward or punishment" approach to motivation does not work over the long term. There is compelling research indicating it has the opposite effect, such as stifling creativity, diminishing performance, and fostering short-term thinking. People notice when they are being manipulated to support someone else's agenda. (Of course, in management or other types of conversations, an agenda is often required;

consider the ways in which parents need to teach children boundaries, for example.) There is a time to lead and a time to manage, and not every conversation is a coaching conversation. However, the way to achieve greater results with those you support is to focus on them and their agenda –whether you want to increase sales or develop engaged leaders within your organization and improve business results. So how do you move away from the carrot-and-stick approach? I'm not suggesting that incentives are never good for increasing employee motivation or to help spike sales. Leaders who like incentives to increase their team's performance can be successful at it in the short term. I'm proposing motivating individuals to achieve deeper, meaningful results that have a lasting impact. Motivating them in this way will attract, retain, and engage both aspiring leaders and seasoned leaders over the long term.

In *Drive: The Surprising Truths About What Motivates Us*, Daniel Pink looked at 40-50 years of research in behavioural science and found that intrinsic motivations, specifically in autonomy, mastery, and purpose, are what drive behaviour *(47).*

"We cannot solve our problems with the same thinking we used when we created them." – Albert Einstein

Coaching takes a similar approach. Here's how:

Begin by moving the conversation from telling to asking. As I explained in chapter 1, this requires shifting from a directive approach to an engaging one that encourages people to find their own solutions that work for them and their time frame.

We are all leaders with our own unique strengths, values, and motivations. When you ask, rather than tell, you begin to draw these strengths out in yourself and others. When my CEO locked us into the boardroom for three days, she didn't tell us how to achieve the task she set out, or problem-solve it for us. She asked us questions about how we could accomplish the impossible and, in the process, we summoned our own unique strengths required for the tasks.

As I've shared, extraordinary leaders learn how to lead from the inside out.

This means drawing out what's inside of you. Do you know what motivates you? Are you aware of your unique strengths and values? If you're not sure, hang in there. I'm going to help you identify them.

Every star performer or HIPO (HIgh POtential) has an underlying motivation for their desire to succeed. What motivates you to be a high achiever? What conditions make it easy for you to reach your goal?

Your mission is to uncover what these motivations are for you and for those you lead.

So how do you uncover what motivates your team?

Take a coach approach.

1. Listen deeply
2. Be curious
3. Ask powerful questions that inspire motivation, meaning and purpose
4. Help your team create a plan (their plan)
5. Provide ongoing support

If you're looking for a silver bullet in this book, here it is. Coaching works! *Getting support from the right coach is one of the main reasons why coaching works.* People experience far greater success with ongoing, appropriate support. We know that training alone increases productivity rates by 23%. When coupled with coaching, productivity rates increase to 88% *(Arnold 15-16).*

A global study of coaching clients conducted by PricewaterhouseCoopers and the Association Resource Centre found that the return on investment for professional coaching was an average of seven times the initial investment, with more than a quarter of coaching clients reporting an ROI of 10 to 49 times. *(Symonds)*

Another recent study, by MetrixGlobal, LLC, found that professional coaching consistently provides high ROI, in the range of 700%, and that 77% of respondents at a Fortune 500 company reported experiencing a significant positive impact from coaching, with productivity and employee satisfaction being impacted the most. Customer satisfaction also improved significantly, suggesting that happier employees lead to happier clients *(Parker-Wilkins).*

Among the many benefits of coaching is the less obvious but no less significant impact on health and well-being. This was certainly true in my experience, and the studies I share in the following chapters further prove these life-changing benefits. My brother's tragic death made me sit up, take notice, and make a change. The combination of his death and the influence of coaching inspired me to learn more about diabetes, health, and self-care. Coaching taught me the power of presence, and how to listen and be mindful with myself and others. Our bodies send us signals about our health and well-being, but we need to be fully present in order to notice and interpret them. His death triggered questions of "what if..." and a desire to learn how the power of presence might help others with diabetes (and other ailments) as well as the people supporting them.

A study performed at Duke University found that diabetes patients paired with a coach over the phone for 6 months experienced significant improvement in their health. As they tapped into their underlying motivations and behaviours, their adherence to their medications also significantly improved, which, in the long run, increases their life span *(Smith, et al)*.

A similar study found that coaching over the phone with high-risk patients improved various aspects of their health (often within 6 months), including stress levels, eating habits, exercise, physical and emotional health, and readiness to make change. In addition, coaching helped 89% of patients reach at least one of their health goals, ranging from getting better sleep to improving overall quality of life. These are not surprising statistics to me. When integrated with the health field, coaching naturally shifts the health model to a client-centric one, which empowers the patient, keeps them engaged, and supports them to change their lifestyle and better manage their health conditions. Although more research needs to be done on the cost-effectiveness of coaching in the medical field, these preliminary results show huge potential and suggest a positive ROI for hospitals and health care providers *(Lawson, et al)*. Imagine how much less congested emergency rooms could be with a little coaching to help patients become self-responsible.

Coaching has far-reaching impact and isn't industry specific–anyone can reap the benefits. Simply put, coaches not only unleash potential in others, we also help them by eliciting solutions and strategies from within themselves.

Closing the Gap

Coaches are trained to listen, provide growing-edge feedback (area of opportunity), and customize the client's approach to their individual needs, motivations and aspirations. Coaches know that the client is naturally creative, resourceful, and whole, thus they draw out the client's internal wisdom. Coaches facilitate internal shifts and personal transformations that lead to extraordinary results. They help people achieve the impossible. This is particularly true when people want to do something they've never done before, and therefore are unable to call upon any previous success strategies or lessons learned. Coaches help people close the gap between their current and future state. They help them stay on track, often by pulling them out of the minutiae of day-to-day distractions to stay focused on their goal.

Clients involved in a coaching relationship gain traction and overcome obstacles infinitely faster than if they were simply trying to work things out alone, which is challenging to do. It takes longer to make decisions, or get any traction at all, when we are thinking alone in our heads. Sharing our thoughts with an accountability partner (a coach) is a productive way to process. Our awareness is heightened, and we can more clearly discern whether these thoughts are worth pursuing. Our words become "live" once we speak them out loud. In that moment, our thoughts and ideas (formally only internal) become tangible and real. We can also notice old beliefs that are holding us back from achieving our goals. We eventually ask ourselves the right questions, and that's how we start to live our life with intention and mindfulness.

Most people underestimate their own capabilities and often lack confidence to move beyond their current state. You've heard the expression, "what got you here won't get you there." Skills alone can only take you so far. It's not the "how-to" that stops you from moving beyond your current state. Are you ready to hear this? (It might come as a bit of a shocker.) It is your resistance to change and lack of a place where you can be vulnerable and say what you need to say. Coaches help you close this gap between feeling stuck in a rut and excelling beyond what was once imagined impossible. As your confidence grows, momentum builds and anything is possible.

Engaging with a professionally trained coach on a consistent basis (for 6 to 12 months or more) yields the best results. Many clients continue for 2 or more years. One of the long-term benefits of working with a coach is that you develop the ability to coach yourself. You become more aware of your actions, reactions, or inaction and are able to step back from your situation to look at it objectively.

The challenge is, people often don't know how or where to find support. Even when we do find it we're afraid of the unfamiliar. Change is unknown and that can feel scary. We all struggle with the stories we tell ourselves, and for the most part, we tend to buy into our stories unless someone (supportive) challenges us on them.

Who consistently has your back and reminds you of what you are capable of (even when you have lost sight)?

Changing behaviours and mindset is possible, and it takes time. Coaching conversations can spark an inner awakening, helping you separate your thoughts from your awareness. That's where the transformation begins–the journey to living your biggest life.

The Heart of Coaching

The heart of coaching is in the conversation, which takes time, training, courage, and commitment from organizations, leaders, and aspiring coaches. This is easier said than done in today's environment of constant change.

Coaching conversations are where breakthroughs happen and "impossible" futures are declared possible. The coach shows up fully present and committed to the client's success. The person being coached walks away with new insights, inspired and committed to action.

The client chooses the focus of the conversation, while the coach listens, asks powerful questions, and holds up the sign post of the client's end goal. These are not light, fluffy conversations filled with ideas and empty positivity. They have substance, delve into areas that hold the client back, and illuminate possibilities. It's a process of respectful inquiry and a partnership based on trust. The interaction between coach and client/coachee provides clarity to situations and moves the client forward in a powerful way.

The coach holds up the mirror for the client by reflecting back what they hear. Coaches take risks by providing feedback when they hear or observe a disconnect between what the client wants and their behaviours. Most of us are conditioned to avoid sensitive topics all together. My father would say "do not upset the apple cart" when he wanted to protect me from creating unintentional conflict. What I learned from hearing that feedback (more than once) was the value of diplomacy. Challenging the status quo is part of what I do. What's most important is the *how*. Coaches don't ignore crucial issues that have been swept under the rug or pretend that problems don't exist when they do. Often the subjects that feel most awkward and uncomfortable are the ones that need airing out the most. Coaches discuss the undiscussable; always safe but not always comfortable.

Feelings have traditionally been a taboo topic in the workplace. Coaches, however, understand that feelings are at the heart of all human interaction. They are trained to probe below the surface of people's actions and inactions, exploring beliefs and emotions that underlie behaviour. We can't change behaviours if we don't understand the motivation or thinking behind them. Consider the iceberg metaphor. What we see is only a small percentage of the whole. Most of the ice lies beneath the water. Similarly, behaviours are what people do (what we see on the surface), while their motivations, values, beliefs, and perceptions are generally hidden from view.

THE ICEBERG METAPHOR

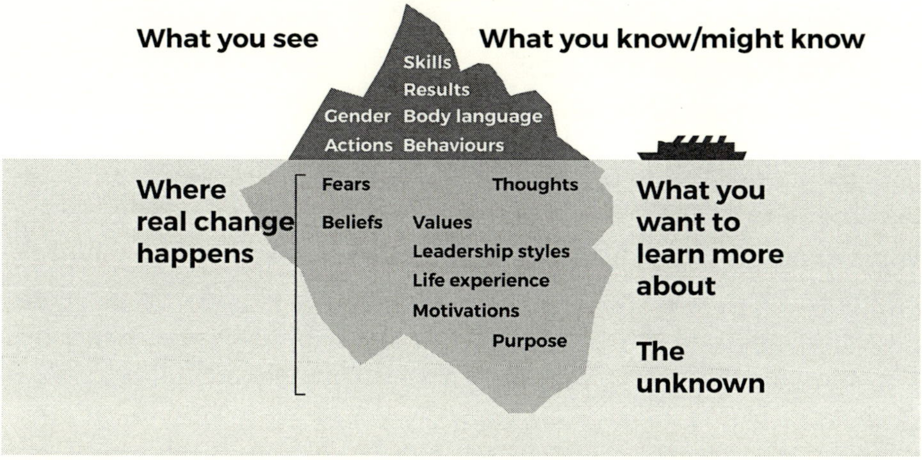

This is actually the yummiest part of coaching. It's where the gold lies, beneath the surface. When we (coaches) learn how to go below the surface, we get to uncover what's at the heart of human motivation. Coaches do this by creating a safe space where clients can be open, vulnerable, and say what they need to say. By asking powerful questions coaches gain greater insight and challenge limiting beliefs.

How does a coach know what powerful questions to ask?

Professional coaches are trained in the skill of asking questions, powerful ones that are truth-seeking and explore their client's inner world. Coaches skillfully use their intuition and curiosity with each coachee as they bring their personal feelings, perceptions, experiences, and inner wisdom to the conversation. Together, this provides the fertile ground where richer, meaningful conversations are cultivated. Moving to action too quickly will throw the conversation off track and address only the tip of the iceberg. When you learn how to probe beneath the water to explore the unseen part of the iceberg, real change can happen.

A coach can also discern behaviour patterns and help the coachee see them as well. By reflecting on the coachee's patterns of thinking and behaving, a coach can help them become aware of what's getting in their way, such as their automatic responses. This new awareness empowers them to make informed intentional choices and take a different approach in the future.

A coach supports clients to develop a strategy that works for them. Often, we will choose a solution that does not align with our goals or values because it's the easiest or quickest path forward (at least we think it is). Coaches act as a sounding board and can help clients see how their decisions align (or not) with their goals and values, and then guide them to make intentional, less reactive decisions.

Coaches help coachees find their own path. Let's face it; we all have great ideas about how to help people, and telling them somehow makes us feel important and valued. That is *not* coaching. We can hinder our coachees progress and knock coaching off track by telling them how we think they need to do something (based on our agenda or how we did it in the past). Making assumptions about what they need to do or know wastes valuable time, money, and energy. Coaching is not mentoring or consulting. Unless we are asked our opinion (yes, I know it's really hard to keep quiet!), our well-intentioned problem-solving gets in the way. We also send the message that we don't really believe the coachee is capable or even smart enough to find their own path forward. This type of interaction hinders the creation of new thinking patterns, which occurs when we tap into the prefrontal cortex of the brain.

If, on the other hand, we stick to asking questions that empower clients to find their own solutions, they will generate new neural pathways that lead to new thoughts, behaviours, and, ultimately, a new mindset. The deeper your questions go, the deeper your client must sort through their own brain to find the answer. The deeper their sorting is, the more powerful their change can be.

Today there is an overwhelming number of highly capable people in all walks of life and leadership levels who are so busy they often don't think for themselves. Not because they can't, but simply because they don't take time within their day to step back, reflect, and set their intention. Coaching conversations help us do this.

Most of us were raised to look to someone else for answers. The reality is we have the answers within ourselves. Applying a coach approach (the skill of asking questions) helps us think for ourselves and search for our own solutions. When we look within for answers, we stop relying on others, which frees up time for them and clears space for creativity. The more we seek within (rather than being told the answer), the more we learn to trust ourselves. Everyone has unique experience, which is why receiving an answer from someone else does not lead us to our inner truth and our best path forward. While the opinions of others can enhance our understanding or inner knowing, the only person who truly knows the best path forward is you.

Let's take a minute to fully take this in. I get it… you may be feeling like you've spent all this time searching, possibly even blaming, to eventually learn, that the answer is within you. Take a big breath in and release.

All of the external noise can confuse our understanding of what is best for us. Obviously at times we do need to consult, gather facts, receive guidance, and brainstorm ideas. However, not searching within for our own answers has far-reaching consequences and perpetuates our preconditioned behaviour of seeking answers outside of ourselves.

Asking others to solve our problems is a deeply rooted behaviour that influences many aspects of our lives and requires a profound shift.

Coaching conversations demand the investment of quality time in people at all levels of an organization or in your coaching business. When coaching is part of an organization's culture, these conversations occur consistently. They are not biannual conversations between employee and manager to discuss performance, what is and isn't working, whether or not expectations are being met (or the status quo), and how to raise the bar. Organizations that want to keep pace with the speed of change need a much different approach. Evolving human capital requires time, commitment, and the ability to engage others in a more meaningful way.

The Stages of Change

We already know that coaching leads to positive change. However, before entering into a coaching engagement, it's important to understand the several stages of making a change. Understanding these stages is helpful for anyone embarking on any kind of change or supporting others in doing so. Change is a process, and part of that process is understanding one's readiness to move forward, as well as recognizing where someone is on that continuum. The Transtheoretical Change Theory describes a 6-stage process.

1. **Precontemplation:** They're not ready. Others may have suggested several times that they should change. They may not recognize the need to change, or they may be uninformed about the benefits of making change and they tune out or ignore the requests of others.
2. **Contemplation:** They're thinking about taking action and are becoming aware of the changes they need to make. They're open to ideas and beginning to imagine how things could be different, yet they're still undecided.
3. **Preparation:** They're getting ready to take action and feeling more committed to making a change. They intend to take action in the near future or may have already taken a first step by gathering information or signing up for a class. It's normal in this stage to toggle back and forth between preparation and contemplation.
4. **Action:** They're making observable changes and taking positive action.
5. **Maintenance:** They have some confidence in the change they've made and are less likely to revert to old behaviour.

6. **Termination:** The new behaviour has become entrenched. The change has been made, and new pathways have been created in the brain *(Prochaska & DiClemente).*

Professional coaches are trained to listen for which stage of change the client is in and assists the client in progressing through subsequent stages. As I've said, the more clients receive coaching, the more they begin to self-coach between sessions. They begin to challenge their own assumptions, thoughts, and behaviours. This accelerates the changes they are making and leads to adaptive change, which creates new learning and ways of thinking. Why is adaptive change important? We need new ways of thinking when our current skills do not solve the problem and what we've done in the past is no longer getting results. These types of changes are difficult because they require breaking old habits and creating new ones. If you have ever tried to break a bad habit–quitting smoking, for example, or adopting healthier eating habits–you know how hard this is.

Coaches facilitate the transformation of our thinking and behaviour, which leads to new way of being. Robert Hargrove describes this process of transformation as "triple loop learning" *(120).*

Here is an example of triple loop learning applied to coaching:

Single Loop: Providing a tip or technique to guide someone's actions. (Coaches who aren't professionally trained often coach here.)

Double Loop: Creating awareness, reframing people's mental models, and empowering them to think differently. With professional coach training you can expect to begin coaching here.

Triple Loop: Altering a person's way of being. The person's thinking and behaviour are transformed. The person who is present now was not there before. The person who was there before no longer exists.

With many hours of professional coach training and lots of practise and feedback from a professional mentor coach, you, too, can develop your skills and experience triple loop learning for yourself, as well as facilitate this change in others. After more than a decade coaching hundreds of leaders to increase performance, this is where I have found the gold in coaching. It doesn't get better than this. It's also what makes coaching the best profession in the world!

Being an Extraordinary Coach–an "Inside Job"

People often believe that being a great coach is about being an expert, or that it involves giving advice or answers. You know by now that the opposite is true. Coaching is a commitment to:

1. Giving people the gift of your presence.

2. Inspiring them toward their BIG Vision.

3. Co-creating extraordinary results.

One day, after several flights with my husband, who was piloting a Cirrus SR22, he asked me if I wanted to try flying. I eagerly agreed (with a little apprehension and plenty of fear as I observed the view below us). After that brief experience, it occurred to me that flying a plane is a lot like coaching. Admittedly, it's a little more complex, especially when you're at 8,000 feet, but they share some common principles. Flying demands sifting through an enormous amount of information coming at you (just like coaching, only you're typically on the ground!), yet you really don't have to work very hard. Gentle touches on the trim tab (the mechanism used for making small adjustments) will help point the plane in the right direction, keeping it on course. Extraordinary coaches know that it's often the smallest tweaks that make the greatest difference in keeping themselves and their clients on track. Flying, like coaching, requires you to be fully present with what's happening in the moment, both from an internal perspective (thoughts, fears, assumptions, and intuition) and an external one (flight instruments, air traffic control, aviation weather). Being present helps you navigate where you are going, stay on course, and achieve results. And, in the case of flying, it's all about arriving safely.

I've talked about leading from the inside out. Coaching itself is also an "inside job." That is, when we coach others, it is as much about how we cultivate our internal resources (including intuition) as it is about accessing it in those we coach.

Have you ever experienced frustration when asking a team member to do something? You told them *how* to do it, yet time and time again it still doesn't get done. How frustrating is that? I get it. I've been there. It's what I refer to as "repeat business" (the wrong kind). Your door keeps opening and you are up against the same conversation over and over again. Or perhaps a team member tells you they want to do something, but they don't, no matter how much encouragement you give them. You struggle to find ways to effectively motivate them. Have you found yourself in a similar situation, where you really want to achieve a goal but just can't seem to make it happen? People around you are saying go for it, but you can't quite figure out how?

Traditional leadership styles employ a "blame or explain" technique, meaning they blame the employee or explain the process to the employee in a different way, so that maybe next time they will do it right. Too often this doesn't produce the sought-after results.

Learning to step back and observe the whole picture, before approaching others for the second or third time about a single issue, will allow you to adjust your approach, to instead explore what's beneath the surface. A coach will reflect on the situation and try to understand his/her own impact. For example, ask yourself;

How am I contributing to these results?

What in me needs to change?

How might I approach this differently?

Rather than blame or explain, reflecting or self-coaching will help you approach the conversation with a greater awareness and curiosity about the situation. More importantly, when you learn how to apply a coach approach and ground yourself in the conversation, you are better able to provide the coachee the gift of presence. Giving someone this gift of presence is powerful. People will notice you're right there with them–and that you bring your whole self to the conversation, remaining non-judgmentally, fully present as you explore what's going on beneath the surface of the unintended result.

Leaders using a coach approach must continually sharpen their own saw as well. By receiving coaching on their own challenges and opportunities, they are better equipped to help others achieve their "impossible" future and co-create extraordinary results.

Coaching is about co-creating extraordinary results by nurturing and inspiring the human spirit.

The Importance of Aligning Your Values

As I shared earlier, there was a period of time in my corporate career when I became extremely frustrated and began to second-guess my leadership ability. The company I worked for was in decline, and I had exhausted all the tools I had to support leaders in growing themselves, their teams, and their business units. While I continued to support others on their journey, I didn't have anyone to support me on mine. I had peers and managers, but I didn't have a coach.

After many years of doing what I loved, coaching and training, my role began to change. I later realized that my values were no longer aligned with my role or the company. Even though coaching was part of my role, it wasn't part of the corporate culture, which used a hierarchical, top-down approach. As the axe came down on more jobs, trust and security eroded. Our think tanks and brainstorming sessions led to unclear expectations and much less desirable outcomes. It became increasingly risky for anyone to name the "elephant in the room" or express how they actually felt. The result was mediocrity. The downward spiral ensued, which resulted in Chapter 11. It was a case of the boiling frog dilemma, and it happened in front of my eyes. Because the threat increased gradually over years, management didn't realize they were in hot water until it was too late.

Thankfully, I followed my intuition and attended the graduate-level coaching program, which helped me understand why I had been feeling so discouraged. Although it came naturally to me and I had experienced success coaching leaders, I did not have a clearly defined process or a deeper understanding of what is behind human motivation. The program taught me this, and how to get to the best out of myself and others. I also experienced the value of receiving support.

Perhaps the most valuable insight (although I already knew at a visceral level) was that my love of learning was not being met, which meant I wasn't growing. Intuitively I knew I needed something more. It was this feeling that led me to apply to the graduate program in the first place.

Have you ever tolerated something that went against who you are and what you stand for? What did that feel like? For me, at first, it felt as though I were driving a car with two flat tires and getting nowhere fast. Eventually I felt as though something deep in my core was being chipped away.

This was also the case for a senior VP who shared with me that a small group of elite executives (including him) received 80% of the bonus pool for his company. While this enabled people at his level to buy beautiful homes and live opulent lifestyles, he found the system unfair and abusive. There was zero transparency in the organization. He was surrounded by decisions that were out of his control and didn't line up with his values. His inner voice was shouting at him, "This is not right!" He realized that, ultimately, if he was going to be happy he could not ignore that voice. Two of his core values, integrity and fairness, were not being upheld at the company. Money wasn't enough to keep him there. He handed in his resignation and began a new career where he felt aligned with his strengths and values, thriving in ways beyond the size of his paycheque.

Another client, a VP in her organization, described a culture where finger pointing, judging, and subtle rudeness were common at senior-level meetings. There was no sense of support or company values that would allow her to feel safe enough to speak her mind. She held back her opinions and ideas for fear of not being liked, being seen as pushy, or being the subject of the week's water-cooler conversation. This person was naturally a great communicator and a high achiever, yet she could not bring her whole self into meetings with her peers. The irony hit home when her bosses recommended that she should be bolder and more courageous. They weren't aware that they themselves were part of the issue by failing to create a safe space for employees to fully show up. Her values collided with the culture they had created. Coaching empowered her to step up and speak out.

When our lives don't align with our values we feel that inconsistency in our body; we feel stressed and off balance. Once you are clear on your values, goals, and purpose, you can live a happier, more fulfilled life because you can make conscious choices to boldly align your decisions, actions, and successful habits with your priorities. Imbalance happens when we are not aligned, and while it may sound simple, finding alignment is a process.

Thankfully, coaching helps us uncover all of this and get clear on what's important.

Let me be clear; sometimes it takes more than an internal nagging sense of discomfort to get us moving in the direction we need to go. Sometimes an external force beyond our control is the catalyst to creating a big shift in our life, causing us to redefine our future. That's often what it takes when we feel stuck and too afraid to make a change.

It's interesting how life has a way of sending us messages. The messages often start off quiet but get louder if we don't listen. I had a loud awakening while at a hotel in Kelowna, British Columbia. In the middle of the day I heard several loud gunshots, followed by screams. I jumped up to look out my 10th-floor window, where I watched people fleeing for cover or dropping to the ground. I then heard another stream of shots from what sounded like an automatic weapon. The lake view, which had been filled with white sails and people walking along the boardwalk, was suddenly empty. It was eerie and frightening. My amygdala (the part of the brain responsible for the fight, flight, or freeze response) kicked in and my body went into shock.

I thought, *Now what!* Was this an isolated shooting or someone on a rampage? I didn't know if I had one minute or one hour to live! I phoned the hotel's front desk and was told to stay in my room, away from the windows. We were in lockdown. Next, I heard the scream of sirens. I felt powerless, like a sitting duck, with terrifying thoughts running through my head. I picked up my mobile and contacted friends and family to let them know what was happening.

Eventually the lockdown was lifted and we were free to leave our rooms. I ventured downstairs and began engaging the staff to hear about their experiences. They had hidden in freezers and under the bar. It was terrifying for them. Several shared with me that the experience it was a life-changing event, and I could hear in their voices how it was causing them to reassess their lives. (Once you're trained as a coach, you bring a coach perspective everywhere you go!)

So what was my takeaway? The experience was a *loud* reminder that we never know when our time is up. I knew I needed to finish my book and get my message out there! And this is my message: If you are not following your heart and building your dream, what are you waiting for? Listen to your inner voice. You know the one that keeps tapping you on the shoulder saying, "Hello, are you listening?" It's important that we pay attention to our internal wisdom, our intuition or gut feeling. We don't always do so, because we don't make a habit of trusting it. When it arises we question if it's real. Or we think we have more time so we wait and procrastinate.

I hope that you'll take the opportunity right now to begin (or strengthen) a habit of trusting your intuition so that it doesn't have to put you in lockdown to get your attention!

Are you ready for reflection and a little journalling?

Trusting Your Inner Wisdom

Reflection

Are you aware of the internal wisdom speaking to you from within?

If so, can you think of a time when you heard it? What did it tell you?

____

Did you follow it? ____

____

What happened as a result? ________________________________

____

Now, think of a time when you didn't follow your gut? What happened?

____

Identifying Your Core Values

Reflection

Let's continue our discussion on the importance of aligning yourself with your values. Make a list of the 5 values that matter most to you.

Here are some values to get you started:

Success	Thoroughness	Winning	Integrity
Flexibility	Harmony	Creativity	Collaboration
Transparency	Accountability	Happiness	Innovation
Taking Risks	Fairness	Respect	Autonomy
Competition	Growth	Trust	Openness
Health	Supporting Others	Developing Others	Process
Team Work			

1. ____
2. ____
3. ____
4. ____
5. ____

Are your top 5 values aligned with your career, goals, relationships, etc.?

If not, what needs to shift? ____________________________

____

____

____

Change Begins with You

Aligning your goals with your values and your strengths helps you feel happier, healthier, and more productive. It's not easy to do, however, because it requires focused effort and time to reflect on what's important. This is the adaptive change I talked about earlier, which does not happen overnight. Adopting new thinking and behaviour patterns and creating new neural pathways in the brain takes effort and support. That's where a professionally trained coach makes the difference. Over a period of time, he/she can help you bust through limiting beliefs and stories you "sell" yourself that keep you from following your heart's path.

So many of our old stories and beliefs simply do not serve us. For example: "I can't leave my job. How will I support my family if I can't find another one?," "I can't build my own business. What if I'm not successful?" I've certainly told myself similar stories. I tried to sell myself on the idea that I couldn't leave the corporate world because I was a single parent and needed the income to support my three young children. It became such an integral part of my belief that I even "sold" that story to some of my closest family and friends, who bought it. I almost bought it too, although deep down I wasn't convinced. I was, however, afraid. The risk of not being able to support my children financially truly frightened me. So I hired a coach. I shared my story and my goals. She didn't buy my story. Instead, she recognized that my real hurdle was fear of the unknown, and she helped me create a plan for my future vision. The rest is history.

Of course, I haven't "arrived" in any final sense. We never actually do, because life is a learning journey. You have proof, however, that I didn't buy into my limiting stories–you wouldn't be reading this if I had! The stories (we make up) are present for all of us, and with each new ceiling we push through, a new fear shows up and a new story is created. ("I can't write a book....who am I? I'm not a writer," and so on.) I'm thankful for the internal wisdom, the ability to self-coach, and the knowledge of the difference between what is real and what is perceived. My hope is that by reading this book, you will achieve this knowledge in your own life too.

The learning journey continues. We must continue to grow, renew, and reassess. That's why hiring a coach helps move us to the next level of success. This book wouldn't have been possible without my own book coach. She kept me on track and helped me move forward, even during the most difficult days when I had limited hours (and no shortage of excuses) to focus on this work. Even when I felt as though I was letting her down, she showed up without judgment, solely focused on what I needed in order to make headway. Often it was just a matter of listening to me talk through all the pressure I put on myself to finish this book in time for my deadline. I was frequently reminded that, along with my goal of publishing this book this year, I was keeping all my other plates spinning at the same time. I was working in and on my business, building and delivering accredited coach training and business development programs for coaches and leaders, coaching leaders and teams, rebranding, launching a new website and, of course, carving out time for my beautiful family and vibrant personal life. Was it easy? No. Did I do it? Yes!

I have learned that life is a journey, not a destination, and stories are just that; stories. We can simply observe them, adopt them, or remind ourselves they aren't true unless we let them be.

Reflection

What goals or aspirations have you accomplished? ______________

____

What big challenges have you overcome? ______________

____

____

What do you know now about yourself? ______________

____

____

What else did you learn? ______________

____

____

What's possible for you in the next 12 months? ______________

____

____

____

When we first start practising new skills, habits, and behaviours with the goal of creating significant, lasting change, the process can feel clunky or choppy, and we will likely revert to our old comfortable behaviours. With repetition, however, the process becomes smoother and creates the lasting change we want. Working with a coach helps us focus on the thoughts and actions needed to gain the greatest traction. It is clear that what we focus on grows, and if we listen to our stories for any length of time, we tend to buy into them. A coach can reflect these thought patterns back to us to help us hear our own words. With this insight we can identify our truth, and start owning what we truly want for our lives. That's the power of coaching!

Clearing the Path for Change

One afternoon I was clearing a vine that was twisted around a very large Rose of Sharon tree in my yard. This vine had tightly woven its way around, up, and down the trunk and branches of the tree. When I got closer I saw that the tangled vine was hundreds of feet long, choking the tree, almost taking it over. It took me hours to remove it completely. Within days of being freed, the tree experienced exponential growth, blooming vibrantly, as if to say, "Thank you, I can breathe again!"

This is a metaphor for something we all need at times in our own lives. We need to clear the path for what's to come. We need to untangle the vines that crowd our view and stifle our ability grow so that we can bloom again. Free of restrictions, we can take our career, business, and life to extraordinary heights.

What vines need clearing in your life so that you can breathe freely and grow more vibrantly?

Moving On

Throughout my life, awakening has come at times of deep sadness or great stress caused by external factors. At these times big shifts occurred. For instance, while I was stopped in my tracks by the sheer grief and sadness of losing my youngest brother, opportunities arose in the space created by these dark moments. Courage calls us forth during the most challenging times of our lives. With courage and strength, we can rise above those challenges to make the changes we need most.

Change caused by external factors necessitates time for healing, reflection, and just being. It is in these pivotal moments that our lives are redefined. Having time and space to think is paramount when something big has shifted in our lives. When we suffer loss such as death, downsizing, or divorce, we may find ourselves in a fog. We might simply go through the motions, day by day. All we can do is get out of bed, put one foot in front of the other, and wait until the fog lifts and we can begin to see clearly. We emerge changed by the experience. We are new again; stronger, more resilient, and with a deeper sense of who we are and what's important.

Whether you have suffered a recent loss or are experiencing a challenge right now, give yourself the gift of time to recharge and do more of what you love. Take a walk on the beach, meditate, take creative cooking classes, travel, go to the theatre. Get out there and experience all that life has to offer. Bring yourself into a creative space as often as you can. That is where clarity and innovation happen. Ask for help. Get support where needed. You don't need to do it all alone.

"The growth and development of people is the highest calling of leadership."
– Harvey S. Firestone

Chapter 5

Leading with a Coach Approach

The Art and Science of Human Motivation

Firestone's quote is the essence of this book. For today's leader, the growth and development of people is no longer just one option on the road to success. Instead, it's an essential habit required by all leaders, managers, and influencers. This means regularly scheduled development conversations secured in your calendar day to day, week to week (not just when time permits), and requires foundational coaching skills as part of your tool kit.

We all have so much potential in our lives, and as leaders, it is our responsibility to help those we support tap into theirs. Harnessing potential helps people feel more energized and is vital in order for leaders and organizations to thrive. However, much of a team's potential remains dormant because coaching is rarely prioritized as a key leadership strategy. I listened to Sir Ken Robinson's keynote speech at an ICF conference years ago. He too talked about how the untapped potential left undeveloped around the world is quite sad. Coaching helps to turn that around. When we coach others, we tap into their potential and make impossible futures possible.

Developing Coaching Cultures

"All companies have a culture. Some companies have discipline. Few, however, have a culture of discipline. When you have disciplined people, you don't need a hierarchy. When you have disciplined thought, you don't need bureaucracy. When you have disciplined action, you don't need excessive controls. When you *combine a culture of discipline with an ethic of entrepreneurship, you get the magical alchemy of great performance" (Collins 13, italics mine).*

Discipline in a basic sense can be taught and modelled, but true discipline, which Collins speaks of here, comes from within. When employees are motivated internally (not externally by carrots and sticks), aligned with their values and goals, and doing work that they are passionate about, they experience greater performance. Employees want to contribute to their company's success, especially when they feel valued for their unique contribution and can see a clear connection to their own goals and values.

In fact, when coaching skills are applied as part of an organization's culture, employees and management teams alike help each other grow and progress. Performance reviews become irrelevant because coaching conversations become the mechanism for goal-setting and ongoing feedback. When this becomes a consistent leadership habit, organizations produce extraordinary results. I've experienced this firsthand. Notice I use the term *ongoing*. Coaching conversations are not a one-time event. To be effective, coaching needs to become a regular part of a manager's role. It is a continual process without an end date.

Organizations that apply coaching as a leadership strategy also understand that coaching skills are a key competency for leaders at all levels. The coach approach is modelled by its leaders. It becomes part of their DNA. It is an instinctive part of who they are and how they lead.

There are plenty of one- or two-day coaching programs that teach coaching techniques, provide personal development, or offer tools for improving leadership skills. Some of these one-off workshops can be valuable for shifting mindsets and inspiring new thinking. When leaders return to work, however, they find it difficult to integrate their new knowledge into the busyness of the day-to-day. Before too long, they find themselves right back where they started. The knowledge they acquired may have been insightful, but if there is nothing in place to anchor the learning, all the inspiration and good intentions quickly fall away. For lasting impact and real change to occur, training needs to be coupled with coaching. We can compare this problem to buying a car without the wheels. You're not going to get very far.

Again, leading with a coach approach requires leaders to be equipped with core coaching skills. They learn the foundations of how to build trust, empower others, and see their employees as resourceful and capable. As Jim Collins says, "Good to great companies built a consistent system with clear constraints but they also gave people freedom and responsibility within the framework of that system" *(225).*

In other words, the freedom to be creative, combined with an entrepreneurial spirit within the system (or intrapreneur) equals innovation. Leaders are equipped to be great coaches, and those who consistently apply a coach approach with their teams experience far greater results, as I've shared.

Unfortunately, most leaders are not trained or skilled in coaching techniques. If they are, too often the inspiration or discipline is lost. If all leaders experienced the value of coaching, I think everyone would be doing it. Once people catch on to the power of coaching to unleash human potential, it will become what they "do." For now, those on the leading edge (as the case studies in this chapter will illustrate) are reaping the benefits of coaching already. We also know that even coaches need coaching. The decision to train internal coaches in an organization makes coaching more accessible to all levels of leadership and is more cost-effective and sustainable long term.

The Value of Transparency and Confidentiality

Organizations that employ coaching as a leadership strategy develop leaders who engage the hearts and minds of their teams, one conversation at a time. It takes time to develop and practise coaching. The more you practise, the quicker your confidence and momentum build. Let me be clear; business results won't skyrocket overnight. The coach approach is a methodical process that inspires disciplined action and creates a culture of accountability. Over the long-term, organizations that employ this strategy will lead change and innovation into the future.

How exactly do you facilitate change through coaching?

And how does it work?

First, coaching helps keep your finger on the pulse of those you support and become aware of what your coachee is thinking, feeling, and understanding. Coaching is not just about improving performance; it goes much deeper than that. Asking powerful questions generates new thinking, and the coach is an observer to this learning. Done consistently, it greatly enhances leadership capability within an organization.

Second, coaching conversations help wipe away judgment, hierarchy, and biases. This develops heart-centred leaders within the company culture who authentically lead with their heart, not just their head. When people have a place where they can be themselves and share their thoughts, a place they trust, feel safe, and know their conversation will be kept confidential, it allows them to open up fully. (We can apply this recipe to our personal relationships too.)

When a coachee opens up fully, their coach can uncover the root of how their values and beliefs connect to their behaviours (such as negative self-talk), which ultimately affects performance and can lead to disengagement and the resistance to change. With this insight, the coach can further direct the coachee's focus toward positive self-talk and create lasting change. Confidentiality helps cultivate trust, therefore it must be taken seriously and held to the highest standard.

Coachees are deeply aware that their coach has their back, no matter what. Think about it: What would be possible if the conditions for growth were optimal? A coach believes in you and is committed to your growth, no matter what you say or do.

Another key ingredient for facilitating change is transparency. Transparency is vital because it allows us to be authentic, to be ourselves rather than pretend to be someone we're not. Where there is transparency, deep connections can develop. This leads to improved trust, communication, and leadership effectiveness. Without transparency, communication is vague and inauthentic, which leads to unproductive conversations, a big time waster.

When I was a child, I sensed when my parents or family members were keeping something from me. I would ask questions and urge them to tell me what was going on. To quote my husband, "Children are just short; they're not stupid!" As a child, it would frustrate me when adults weren't forthcoming. I was curious and wanted to learn about the nuances of conversation whenever possible. I was (and still am) like a sponge. Now, of course, I realize there's a time and a place for certain conversations. Some topics are not appropriate for children, or the timing isn't right. Some topics were basically none of my business! I had to learn that too.

The point is, we all have internal BS detectors (research confirms this). Our brains alert us when people are not being open and honest, when they're holding something back, when they're offering only partial information or even withholding the truth altogether. Just like when we were children, this can feel confusing and cause uncertainty. We may react to that uncertainty by clamming up, which not only causes communication to suffer, but can erode our relationships over time.

We all have experience with this type of situation–where a lack of trust, perhaps in a work environment, made you feel the need to "watch your back". Cultures of transparency strive for the opposite: an environment that is safe, positive, and nonjudgmental, where people connect on a deeper level, instinctively knowing that they can trust each other and be themselves. An environment where authenticity and trust are the norm is optimal for growth.

Coaches and leaders can model transparency, authenticity, and trust. You may be thinking, "If I'm transparent with others, people will know too much about me, judge me, and that will put my career at risk." I understand that transparency can make you feel vulnerable, but it's the only way to show up fully. Transparency doesn't mean you have to get naked, as in opening up about every aspect of who you are or what's happening in your life, but it does require the courage to speak your truth. When you have the courage to be transparent, you feel more authentic. We feel happier when we honour who we really are.

So how do you create a culture of transparency, authenticity, and trust? I teach this in my coaching programs, and it does grow and develop over time (much like a coaching relationship). For now, let me paint a picture that better describes what I mean. I love this quote by the famous peace clown, Wavy Gravy, who invites us to laugh together and embrace our imperfections rather than resist or be embarrassed by them.

"We are all bozos on a bus. So, sit back and enjoy the ride." –Wavy Gravy

This has impacted me in many ways and is relevant in creating a culture of authenticity, transparency, and trust. Wavy normalized humanity and let us know we are more the same than different. He gives us permission to stop pretending. We all struggle with similar thoughts; we're constantly learning, and yet we think we're alone in the way we feel. We're all "Bozos on the Bus," living in a complex world, working hard to present a self-assured image to each other on a daily basis. Yet we're all born without an instruction book, imperfect and prone to making mistakes. We have all done stupid things that we are ashamed of and have numerous shortcomings. We have all tossed and turned in the middle of the night worrying about everything from our to-do lists and finances to family and negative media.

If we're all just bozos then we can remove the façade and get back to being bozos (a.k.a. who we really are).

> How would it feel to take a more compassionate view and embrace our imperfections?
>
> What if we choose to accept our seat on the bozo bus rather than yearn to be on the "normal" bus with all of the happy, healthy, handsome people who never make mistakes, lose their wallet, or forget where they parked?

We're all on the bus that says BOZO, so take your seat and enjoy the ride.

Holding both perspectives; that we are all "bozos," yet capable of greatness– enables us to soar into amazing possibilities while keeping our feet on the ground and a smile on our faces.

Accountability and Self- Responsibility

Compassion, trust, empowerment, courage, intuition, and transparency are defining characteristics of coaching cultures. While some of these are "soft" skills, a coaching culture is also steeped in accountability and self-responsibility, which support individuals, teams, and organizations in achieving extraordinary results.

We all need someone to be accountable to, especially when we are learning or trying something new, and our confidence is not yet strong. An accountability partner ensures we take action toward achieving our goals and assists us when we find ourselves stuck on fear or self-doubt.

Accountability means that you *Do What You Say You Will Do.* Coaches encourage you to fulfill your commitments as well as *Be Who You Say You Will Be.* Remember, one of the cool things coaching addresses is who we decide to be. When we align the person we aspire to be (and our values) with our actions, we can change unwanted behaviour. When a client or team member commits to a goal or task, the coach's job is to hold his/her feet to the fire. However, as you might have guessed, the process is not quite so cut and dry.

In chapter 4, I shared the six stages of change model that an individual experiences as they move through change. Professional coaches are highly skilled at assessing where their client is at, and they understand the importance of paying attention to it. We are all at different stages of change for different reasons, and at different times in our life. (Thankfully, we're not all in the middle of significant change at the same time!) Thus, we need to be mindful that we don't drag people kicking and screaming into our boat simply because we *think* they need to change (or we want them to). We must first listen for their readiness and support them in their process toward change. Pushing hard when they aren't ready will not work, and it will be detrimental to those involved (your team, your loved ones, or your organization). What we ultimately want to infuse is a culture of self-responsibility.

This concept of *readiness* also applies to sales. It's important to assess where your clients are in their readiness to buy from you. It may take several conversations over time before they are ready to move forward. Consistent follow-up creates connection, builds trust, and helps them feel increasingly ready. Readiness is also critical for attaining the buy-in of any individual, team, or organization before one commits to take action toward their goal. If genuine interest is lacking, accountability and self-responsibility won't emerge.

So, with this in mind, how do you obtain buy-in from your team when you have big goals to achieve? Consider *what's in it for them*. Find out how their goals and strengths fit into the company vision. Ask your team what they find important about achieving this goal. Listen for alignment in their responses. Also consider: How does *your* company vision support *their* goals, values, and strengths, if at all? Your job is to help connect the overall team goal with the individual's goal by listening to what gets *them* excited. If you're not sure, ask them. They will tell you.

Your team's motivations determine their behaviour. Therefore, the easiest way to create a culture of accountability–which is all about self-responsibility and action in a timely manner without *pushing*–is to develop deep trust with your team by caring enough to listen to what matters most to them. When their strengths and motivations are linked to your goal, they will be more committed to doing the work. Why? Because they can rally around a goal that has genuine meaning and purpose for *them* too.

I'll share an example from my own experience in growing my business and team. When I started training new staff to help me increase sales and have more impact, I began to feel frustrated when I didn't see results. After exploring the issue with my team, I learned that they felt they were bothering prospects by following up. It did not feel authentic to them. I knew that their internal motivations were very similar to my own: to empower more people to reach their goals so that they can live and lead happier, more fulfilling lives. I realized that I simply needed to reframe their thinking and deepen their understanding of the sales process by teaching them my method, *the coach approach to sales*. During this training process my team realized that by not following up and inviting our prospects to move forward with us, they would risk remaining stuck and not realize *their* goals. Training, coaching, and connecting my team's motivating factors to our company vision was the turning point in achieving greater action and bigger results.

Creating Accountability When Sales Are Down

If you're in a sales role (most of us are in some way, shape or form), you are acutely aware of the need to keep your numbers up. We are only as good as we were yesterday, as the saying goes. So, how do you motivate your sales team without pushing your agenda, especially when sales are down and the pressure is on?

Here are 5 easy tips to guide your conversation with your sales team.

1. It's important to take a moment to step back, breathe, and centre yourself. Preparing yourself for the conversation is essential so that you can show up fully and unattached to your emotions. If you're feeling anxious, frustrated, or angry, it will affect your conversation and have a negative impact.

2. Be curious–find out what your team wants and where they're stuck. Provide context and meaning behind the sales process. What's in it for the client, your team, and the organization?

3. Focus on their strengths and shine light on the positives. Recognize the small wins. This increases confidence, especially when your team begins to second-guess their ability and the "ducks start quacking." You know where this leads.

   Coaching shifts our energy to an upward spiral by focusing on what's possible.

Downward Spiral

Upward Spiral

4. Explore if they are in the "right seat." Are they doing work that excites them? Are their goals aligned with their role? If not, how (or where) can that person bring more strengths to their role?

5. Finally, and most importantly, ask them what they are committing to.

Reflection

Now that you have these tips and tools, how can you engage your sales team to grow in ways that are meaningful for them?

Skills That Support Successful Coaching Cultures

One of the most important skills in developing a coaching culture is the ability to listen. Effective listening means listening on many levels with genuine curiosity without judgment. When we are effectively listening, people feel safe enough to dive deeper into a topic than in your typical boardroom chat.

Often, people think they're fully listening, but most of us are only half listening because we're used to the constant state of distraction. The concerns going on in our own mind, the opinions of others, or what's happening around us are some of the contributing factors to why we half-listen. Can you listen to someone fully without being distracted, forming judgments or opinions, or being preoccupied with your own agenda? Can you be present, in the moment with another person, without daydreaming or wanting to jump in while they are speaking? It's not easy, is it? It requires focus and practise. The first step to being a good listener is to notice when you are distracted. Then become aware of your internal and external distractions. In the next chapter, I'll go into more depth on how to quiet the noise and be more present.

Knowing how to motivate others is also an essential skill. Extraordinary leaders do this. And, to do it well, it's important to learn about one's values and what their passionate about, just as you did in chapter 3. This is critical in empowering your team to do great things. When we're not in alignment with our core values and goals, we fall off track and feel out of balance. The same holds true for the people we support. Part of being aligned is doing meaningful work that connects with our values. You might remember my own experience of when my values weren't aligned with my work. Personal growth is a core value for me. Therefore, when I'm not growing I feel out of alignment, and unsettled. It's normal to feel this way when we aren't paying attention to what's important. It is only when we are truly aligned with our vision and values that we flourish in our careers and in our life.

When I was training to become a professional coach, I needed to practise my newly acquired coaching skills with leaders from diverse business sectors, outside of my own organization and area of influence. Coaching in this new territory brought up huge fear for me initially. I quickly learned, however, that you don't need to have extensive knowledge about a client's profession to be a great coach. You simply need to be equipped with the foundational skills and tools to draw out their knowledge and guide them in the direction they want to go. This is true whether you are leading a small team, multiple business units, or if you are an aspiring coach. You will likely have different life and business experiences than your coachees. That's perfect. You simply need to ask questions to determine what's important to them, coach and support them so they see themselves as resourceful and capable of achieving their dreams.

As I've said repeatedly, the skill of asking questions is key to coaching. Coaches don't set the agenda or provide the answers. The coach is not a know-it-all and they're not there to bestow wisdom. This would be mentoring or consulting (and quite possibly annoying, especially if the person whom you are coaching didn't ask for advice). Occasionally coaches may provide mentoring or helpful information *if it's relevant to the conversation.* This works best when limited, however. A skilled coach will quickly put their coaching hat back on and turn the focus back to the client. Coaches are neutral, curious, and exploratory, and empower the coachee to take BIG action on what they are ready to commit to. Learning how to stay curious and help people take intentional action (not just any action) are important skills in coaching cultures.

When coaches provide answers, they underestimate an individual's (or team's) capability, which can keep them thinking small. There is a world of difference between helping someone step into their potential versus telling them what to do.

A client once shared with me that her boss micromanaged her in a way that felt threatening, with a puffed-up chest and superior attitude. After several coaching conversations with me, she summoned up the courage to provide him with clear feedback indicating that his management style wasn't working for her. This conversation cleared the air instantly. Her manager's intentions were good; however, he was totally unaware that his leadership style was having a negative impact. It was a "rip the blinders off" moment for him. She was "coaching up," which means that by having a courageous conversation, she ended up, in effect, coaching him. She stayed curious about his behaviour and invited him to engage her differently. She made a powerful request by asking him to ask questions rather than charge in with his agenda at every turn like a bull in a china shop.

"Coaching is safe, not always comfortable."
– Marj Busse, Royal Roads University

During my early days as a leader, I also needed to learn to become aware when my own agenda was taking over. I noticed that my body would tense up when this happened, so I learned to step back and take a deep breath. The full transformation occurred when I realized I didn't need to have all the answers. The answers were within my clients, and any agenda must be their own. All I needed to do was tap into their motivation and clear away the clutter (limiting beliefs, lack of confidence, etc.) that was holding them back from their goals. I did not have to push them. In fact, "pushing" slowed the process. The coach's agenda is to help the coachee create their agenda. This is foundational in successful coaching cultures.

Raising the bar and shining a light on what's working, versus focusing on what's not, is ultimately more effective for your client (coachee, team member, loved one). Learning to put your emotions aside, suspend your agenda, and instead ask questions that are curious and nonjudgmental (as opposed to being directive) takes focus, intention, and years of practise. Developing your own awareness as a leader, learning how to listen, ask powerful questions, be present, stay curious, and help your coachee take intentional action are all part of the fundamental skills in setting up successful coaching cultures.

Listening and Trusting Your Inner Voice

Learning to trust your inner voice is also key to becoming a great coach. Learning to listen to yourself before you can listen deeply to others is essential. Also, the more self-aware you are and the better you can navigate your life from the inside out, the more you can help others do the same.

Inner listening involves hearing the little whispers that come from deep within, the ones that nudge and encourage you to take action. Your intuition becomes your inner ears. This idea may feel new for you, and yet it's the single most important lesson in this book–how to lead from the inside out.

There is a saying, "God doesn't call the qualified; He qualifies the called." We all have inside of us something urging us to be greater. If we pay attention and listen to our inner thoughts, or calling, and if we answer that call with a willingness to step out of our comfort zones repeatedly, *this* is precisely what it means to "qualify the called." We are here to make a difference in the lives of others and to grow ourselves. We must listen deeply to what we are called to do, then access our internal power so that we can live fully and reach our greatest potential. This is the internal work of becoming an extraordinary leader.

When coaching others, we listen on many levels. Using intuition, observing nonverbal communication (body language, facial expression, and tone), and being fully present allows us to sense when something else is going on. Just as we listen to our own inner world, we intuit for our clients as well. We listen to their spoken words as well as what's not being said. We must first understand ourselves before we can illuminate others.

Coaching Cultures Return on Investment

Leaders as coaches motivate employees, helping them stay on track and do great work. In organizations where people are encouraged to be authentic, feel empowered, and work with their strengths, accountability and self-responsibility become natural by-products that contribute to extraordinary results.

Over the years I have observed the impact that coaching has on a workplace culture. Several leaders and organizations I have worked with have infused coaching skills into their day-to-day conversations after completing coach training. I've partnered on large scale projects, including with Vancouver-based Essential Impact Inc, where we worked with organizations committed to creating a coaching culture, bringing coaching skills to all levels of leadership.

I have worked with leaders in high-tech, telecommunications, automotive, health care, high-end restaurant chains, and many more. Regardless the industry, I have seen a massive shift in the way leaders engage their teams and the goals they attain as a result of teaching their leaders how to become effective coaches. My clients have shared that my coaching programs have helped them become more aware of their own thinking and motivations, and feel more equipped to coach their managers and the people they support.

I'm fortunate to work with numerous creative, highly skilled, intelligent leaders. I had the honour of working with the CEO of CAA Niagara (Canadian Automobile Association), Peter Van Hezewyk. This is what he had to say:

"Coaching sessions provided a great sounding board and allowed me to focus on the issues at hand and walk away with practical solutions. I've developed more confidence in my leadership approach and I'm beginning to feel more comfortable in coaching as a 'conversation' versus a checklist.

During our executive team coaching sessions, Pam helped us develop greater trust, raise our bar, shift our thinking about leadership and become more effective leaders. We achieved results we had never seen before. We are now coaching our teams, and despite our size, we're leading the way in North America with being #1 in membership growth for all CAA and AAA (American Automobile Association) clubs."

There is plenty of research on the ROI of coaching. In my work as an executive coach, I've had the privilege to work on many game-changing projects. Two in particular involved partnering with organizations that were awarded the ICF International Prism Award in honour of their commitment to applying coaching as a leadership strategy. With its award, ICF recognizes organizations that adhere to the highest standards of excellence while producing outstanding results. Earning this highly coveted award is a big win for recipients as well as for the professional coaching community.

Joey's Restaurants and Rogers Communications were recipients of the Prism award.

Here is some of the ROI organizations have experienced with coaching:

- Double-digit increase in call-centre revenues
- Increased customer satisfaction and decreased number of customer escalations (when a customer demands to speak with a supervisor or someone "higher up")
- 72% improvement in call-centre employee retention
- 682% return on investment (a short 30 months after implementing coach training)
- Reduced staff turnover rate

- Increased speed of decision-making
- Increased membership growth
- Leadership development
- Increased sales
- Reduced sick days

The tangible and intangible results are numerous and clearly indicate that training leaders in coaching skills makes good business sense.

Creating a coaching culture takes dedication and commitment from an organization's leaders, creative thinkers, coaches, managers, and front-line staff. It generally involves bringing in external support, initially to help you develop skill and set up systems for success. Do your research and look for credible, professionally trained coaches who can provide the support you require. Hard work pays off, and the rewards and benefits are worth it. However, the seed of change can start with just one person.

Key Points for a Successful Coaching Conversation

The last chapter offered some of the core concepts of a coaching conversation. We also discussed some of the key characteristics needed to become a coach. I'm going to dive into the components of the coaching conversation itself so you can walk away with a few more tools.

If you plan to attend a coach training program, I recommend carving out blocks of time in your calendar afterward to practise coaching. This will help you embed the skill and create a leadership habit. Coaching needs to be part of a leaders' responsibility and gives the manager time to connect with their team individually and check in on what's working and what's not.

Ideally, coaching skills permeate all levels of an organization, from the way that staff interact with one another and handle day-to-day operational issues to holding regularly scheduled, "formal" coaching conversations. Laser coaching (asking a quick question in the moment) can also be applied daily peer to peer.

I encourage you to do your research and consider attending an accredited coach training program to entrench yourself in coaching skill development. The following key points are not meant to be a substitute for that; instead, they are an overview and guidelines to whet your appetite and hopefully spark your desire to learn more.

Before you begin your coaching conversation, you will want to set up a preliminary conversation with those you're inviting to explore coaching with.

What do they know about coaching? What is their experience, if any? Close any gaps between what they know to be true and what real coaching is. Assess where they are on the scale of readiness to move forward with you. (Please note, if you aren't trained in this area it may be difficult to determine that. Most professional coach training courses will teach you how to do this.)

Here are the key points for successful coaching conversations:

1. **A Private Space.** Find a quiet, private place to speak. Reassure the person that your conversation will be kept confidential (or clarify the bounds of your confidentiality).

2. **Eliminate Distractions.** Be fully present. That may include turning off your mobile phone, forwarding calls to voicemail on your desk phone, logging off from your computer, and explaining to others in your office that you are not to be interrupted.

3. **Make Time.** Give yourself time to complete the conversation. The best coaching happens when people can talk without feeling rushed. If you have a limited amount of time, let the person know, and choose to have a laser-focused conversation in the time you do have.

4. **Listen.** Do this with your ears, your eyes, and your intuition. Notice body language, eye contact, and tone. Show your coachee that you are actively listening, interested, and happy to support them.

5. **Find a Focus.** Once you've got the conversation rolling, help the person to set a reasonable goal for the conversation. You might ask, "What do you want to focus on in this conversation?" This is your opportunity to understand the issues they are facing and what will be of greatest value to focus on. If you have only 20 minutes and your coachee wants to chart a new career path, help them break it down. Find out what part of that topic they would like focus on in the time you have.

6. **Stay Curious.** Ask open-ended questions to help your coachee explore their thoughts and challenges. These questions start with "What" or "How" and pull out information from your coachee. Avoid leading questions such as, "Have you thought about . . .?" as they can pull the coaching off track. Similarly, avoid closed questions, such as, "Do you like what you do?" These questions stop the conversation because they elicit only a yes or no answer.

7. **Stay Clear of Advising.** It's easy to get caught up in advising, and it's best to refrain from it unless the coachee asks specifically for your advice. Storytelling is a good way to offer a new perspective rather than telling them what you think they should do. Remember the story of when my team and I were given the challenge to recruit 1,000 new consultants in one month? I often share this with clients to shift their paradigm when they are faced with obstacles, especially when they're trying to achieve something they never have before. Again, stick to open questions to pull out what the coachee already knows. Remember, your goal is to support your coachee in finding their own path, not to advise them on what path they should take.

   (When you feel the urge to start talking, STOP. Ask a question and imagine that you're stuffing a muffin in your mouth. They will respond while you "chew your muffin" and listen.)

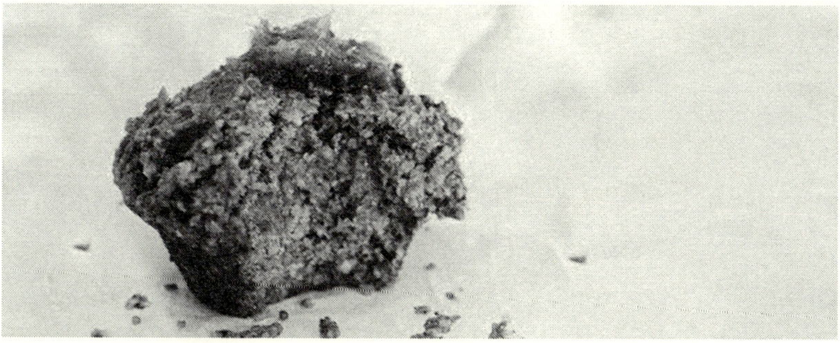

8. **Overcome Obstacles.** In our fast-paced, do-more-with-less work environments, exploring issues before moving to solutions and action is a lost art. Coaching helps the coachee slow down their thinking and explore the underlying issue to overcome obstacles. This ensures you are supporting them to solve the right problem before moving to action.

9. **Provide Authentic Feedback.** Authentic feedback can help your coachees see what they cannot. The coach often notices patterns

(thoughts or behaviours) that are interfering with the coachee's goal. When delivered well, this feedback can be powerful and move the coachee beyond their automatic responses to making more thoughtful choices.

10. **Create an Action Plan.** Ensure that the coachee identifies at least one step or action that they want to take with a time frame to reach their goal. Help them to solidify their plan. Set them up for success, ensuring they have what they need to move forward and will hold themselves accountable. After you complete the conversation, ask for feedback from the coachee regarding what worked and what didn't in the conversation.

Now that you have these 10 key points, let me further distill the 3 elements of a successful coaching conversation: the beginning, middle, and end.

(These key points assume the coachee has agreed to coaching and you have clarified with them what coaching is and isn't.)

Beginning:

- Find a comfortable place and create a safe space.
- Get grounded; turn off all distractions and do what you need to do to clear your headspace and find your zen.
- Set clear boundaries and intention for your time together.
- Focus on setting a goal and outcome for the conversation. What are we talking about today? What do they most need in the time that you have?

Middle:

- Ask open questions. Stay curious. Listen.
- Summarize what you think you heard. This ensures you understood your coachee accurately. It also gives the coachee the opportunity to add to, adjust, and reflect upon what they said.
- Help them see the opportunities and overcome obstacles. Tap into their strengths, knowledge, internal wisdom, and support systems.

End:

- Complete the conversation. Set them up for success.
- Ask them to share their insights and actions. Hold them capable and accountable. Believe in them. Be the holder of their vision even when they lose sight of it.
- Remember to celebrate their wins!

"Between stimulus and response there is a space. In that space is our power to choose our response. In our response lies our growth and our freedom."

– Viktor Frankl

Reflection

What is your new learning?

____

____

____

____

____

____

Revisit these thoughts prior to starting your coaching conversation.

Bottom Line

Coaching works! And, as with any new learned behaviour, it takes practice. Once you learn the basics and engage in coaching conversations, you will hone your skills over time. This book provides you with a taste of coaching and inspiration to dip your toe in the water. There is so much more to learn if you want to be a facilitator of change and have lasting impact.

If you're inspired and ready to further your learning, PGEC offers accredited coach training programs to help you do that. You can flip to the back of the book where I share more!

If you decide to take what you're learning here and apply it without further coach training, remember this: Stay focused on what's most important–leading from the inside out, and in a coaching conversation, helping *the coachee do the same*. It's *their wisdom and their goals*. Help them work on things that will make a difference a year from now. Their success will be your success.

When you lead with a coach approach, you lead from your heart.
It is then that extraordinary things can happen!

Chapter 6

Developing Your Leadership Presence for Lasting Impact

In this chapter, we're going to explore what it means to have a powerful leadership presence, and how to develop yours for lasting impact. We've all met people who possess a powerful presence. We notice something different about them. First, we might notice what's on the outside–the way they show up and how they put themselves together. Then there's the way we experience their presence. They're right there with us; we feel their presence and a deeper connection to them, as though our souls are communicating. This is someone who has mastered the art of full presence, and we leave the conversation changed. These two important dimensions (internal and external presence) create a powerful first impression. People who have cultivated this kind of presence may seem rare and extraordinary. However, it is possible for anyone to develop a presence that people will notice and respect.

By now you know that extraordinary leadership begins from within. To be extraordinary at leading and coaching, it's important to know first how to lead yourself first. That's why I want to bring the focus back to you, to give you the final keys to becoming an extraordinary leader who builds trust and leaves a lasting impression.

Let's start with the external aspects of a first impression. Did you know that you have less than 1 minute to make a good first impression? In fact, people form more than a dozen different opinions about you within the first 10 seconds of meeting you. These are based on your appearance, tone of voice, body language, handshake, the way you dress, and numerous other verbal and nonverbal cues.

We can't help making these snap judgments, which stem from a part of our brain called the limbic system, also known as the emotional centre of the brain. Its functions involve our emotions, motivations, and our memory centre. The amygdala, which is part of the limbic system, is hard-wired to form judgments that strongly influence our behaviour when reacting to stress and fear. I'll elaborate more on this shortly.

So, what exactly are people evaluating, and what assumptions are they making within the first few seconds of meeting you? In part, they are trying to decipher if they can trust you, how smart you are, your level of confidence, and if you're successful.

Most of these areas, which relate to your overall presence, are within your control. For example, people who wear tailored clothing are perceived as successful *(Howlett et al.)*, and those who maintain eye contact while conversing are generally perceived as intelligent *(Murphy)*. The smallest changes can boost your presence and significantly improve how you are perceived, whether you work one-on-one, in small groups, or in front of large audiences. Of course, as a successful executive, leader, manager, coach, or business owner, you have well-developed skills, innate talent, and ability, (that's what got you here), but a powerful presence plays a key role in how you show up.

From her research, Amy Cuddy, a Harvard Business School professor and author of *Presence*, has determined that there are two things people most want to know in the first few seconds of meeting you: Can I trust you? Can I respect you? *(71)*

Why is this important for sales, or the success of an organization? People only want to buy from those they trust and respect. They want to feel that the representative has expertise, knowledge, and capability. Think about it. Would you buy something from someone you didn't trust or respect? Making that determination is part of our internal decision-making process.

So, what does this first-impression research have to do with developing a powerful presence? Everything! Developing a powerful presence is an internal and external practice that requires consistent focus and refinement. Amy shares a very important point that I want to emphasize: We can only exude trust when we learn to trust ourselves first. That is something we cultivate internally. When we learn to trust ourselves, we naturally gain the trust of others.

The Internal Dimension of Presence

As you've read through these chapters, how many times did you feel distracted by your thoughts, a text, a phone call, or someone requesting something from you? Our default is to react when something catches our attention. The ability to live in the present moment is the cornerstone of mindfulness. It includes being aware of our own thoughts and feelings at any given moment.

Mindfulness, or full presence, is the ability to be here now, a skill professional coaches embody and one that requires continual practise. In fact, cultivating mindfulness is the most significant thing you can do to strengthen your leadership presence. This practice will help you lead with wisdom and grace rather than react with anxiety or fear in stressful situations. Mindfulness is what we rely on in order to be present in our own lives and to be in full service of our clients.

Despite the buzz about mindfulness in the business world, to some it may still seem a little "out there." Recent research, however, provides strong evidence that practising mindfulness changes the brain in ways that can benefit everyone, particularly those of us working in today's complex, fast-paced environments.

Psychiatric neuroimaging has shown that just half an hour of daily mindfulness practice (meditation, or a related technique) increases the density of grey matter in areas of the brain that are associated with memory, emotion, empathy, and self-awareness. The result is greater self-regulation, reduced stress, and clearer decision-making. Not to mention enhanced peace of mind *(Marsh)*.

When you practise mindfulness, you develop your "focus muscle," gradually becoming acutely aware of what's happening in the moment and paying attention in a deeper way. This enables you to tune out distractions around you and focus solely and nonjudgmentally on the individual you are engaging in conversation with. The feelings, perceptions, and experiences of others extend far beyond the scope of your own unique lens. When you achieve a mindfulness state, others will feel the gift of your presence, and you'll begin to experience the world in a more meaningful way. This awareness of presence can deepen your conversations, so that you're not just skimming the surface, barely making eye contact and hurrying back to the busyness of your day. As you listen nonjudgmentally beyond the words, you reach beneath the surface of average daily interactions, resulting in richer, more powerful conversations.

I experience this often, most recently while on vacation. I was walking along the beach with my dog one morning when a woman approached me. She was drawn to my golden doodle. (I learned later that she had recently put her own dog down and was saddened by the loss.) She openly shared what was going on in her life. As the conversation came to an end, she thanked me for listening. Later that day, I saw her again. She waved at me and asked for my card. She said that our conversation had made her feel peaceful, and she wanted to learn more about what I do and how I could help her further. I could have made that conversation all about me, but I didn't. I simply listened.

I have met numerous clients this way. Why? Because people want to be heard and are hungry to share their thoughts, deepest fears, challenges, and dreams. When we are present for them, everyone benefits. In fact, our presence is the greatest gift we can offer another person. People can sense when we are fully present or distracted, just as we can sense it in others. Learning how to be present with ourselves helps us be present with others. See how that works? Being fully aware in the present moment with ourselves helps us be in the moment with others. The operative word is *be*. When we learn how to be with ourselves (with practise) this heightens our ability to be with others.

Before elaborating further on how to develop the skill of being present, let's take a moment to review some important and interesting facts about the brain, which add another layer of complexity and potential to your conversations.

What You Need to Know about Neuroscience

The human brain is made of up two key parts. The thinking brain (specifically, the prefrontal cortex) and the emotional brain (the limbic system). The prefrontal cortex, known as the executive, logical part of our brain, is related to analytical, decision -making and problem-solving abilities.

The limbic system is in charge of our emotions. The amygdala (part of the limbic system) is vigilantly on guard against possible threats, and thus helps keep us safe. We have recognized its function since its discovery. (*Burdach, 1819–22).* When the amygdala senses danger, it sends out a signal that activates the fight, flight, or freeze response within a fifth of a second. That signal lets us know in an instant what frightens us, or when something feels unsafe. Additionally, because of our BS detector, which is also located in the limbic system, we know the difference between a surface-level conversation and an authentic one. We recognize when a real connection occurs, even if it only lasts a few seconds. This is coupled with the ability to tap into our intuition, which is thought to be housed in the basal ganglia of the brain. For instance, when someone tries to sell us something and it feels like a scam, it triggers our BS detector. We can then check in with our intuition and decide on the best path forward.

Limbic networks process reward cues just as rapidly as the amygdala processes threats. This provides you with ongoing, nonconscious intuition guiding you toward meaningful outcomes in every situation of your daily life *(Gordon et al.).* In his brain-based model, David Rock says that if we want to know how to motivate others internally, we must understand the true drivers of human social behaviour. For instance, if leaders know that a lack of autonomy activates a genuine threat response, they may consciously avoid micromanaging their employees. As well, they can motivate others more effectively by tapping into internal rewards, such as autonomy, rather than external rewards, such as money or trips to Bermuda *(1).*

Every moment of every day we have a choice to slow down and pause long enough to focus. We can choose to be present despite the distractions of phones ringing, colleagues interrupting, tasks waiting to be completed, our knee-jerk opinions shared out loud, and so on. When we make the choice to slow down, breathe, focus, and be mindful, we calm the amygdala. We become fully present, and in the process our presence is strengthened. Mindfulness is the first step toward tapping into your intuition, which allows you to make decisions in alignment with your values instead of decisions clouded by distraction.

So, if mindfulness brings such benefit, why is it so hard to achieve? Several factors impact our ability to be present. We may not know how to tap into our internal wisdom or even be aware until now that it exists.

- Full presence requires awareness.

- Mindfulness requires practise. It doesn't come naturally for most of us. However, just like going to the gym to strengthen a muscle, when we practise mindfulness, we strengthen our ability to focus.
- Mindfulness requires courage– courage to slow down and be intentional while the world buzzes around us.

Mindfulness Helps Bring Light to Brewing Conflict

To be fully present means that you're present in difficult times too. That can be uncomfortable, and many people find it easier to avoid difficult conversations. When we try to ignore the need for such a discussion, sweeping it under the rug and hoping it will disappear, we merely postpone the inevitable. We tell ourselves that we don't want to create conflict or ruffle any feathers. We think it's easier to stay quiet. However, that avoidance can negatively impact our personal and business relationships, the bottom line and culture of the organizations we work in, even our health.

"On average, each employee spends 2.1 hours each week–approximately one day a month–dealing with conflict in some way... For the US alone, that translates to 385 million working days spent every year as a result of conflict in the workplace" *(CPP Global 3).*

So, the question is not whether conflict can be avoided, but rather how do we deal with conflict more effectively? Do you remember my client who had a conversation with her micromanager? She felt threatened by his demeanour, and while it took courage to provide him with feedback, it was an effective way to handle conflict, rather than avoiding the situation altogether. Avoidance would have made the problem worse, accumulating resentment over time. It would not have given her manager the opportunity to grow from her feedback.

"When channeled through the right tools and expertise, conflict can lead to positive outcomes, such as a better understanding of others, improved solutions to problems or challenges, and major innovation" *(CPP Global 2).*

Yet surprisingly, most employees haven't been trained in effective conflict management. Coaching skills and the skill of asking questions are the most effective tools for dealing with conflict in a productive way.

If you haven't been trained in conflict management or would like to sharpen your skills, a great place to start is with mindfulness. Being mindful and fully present can help us manage conflict by helping us acknowledge the important conversations that need to be had. It can also help us slow down and consider all of the viewpoints in conflict, something we often forget to do.

Have you ever experienced a situation where something felt off? Where do you feel this in your body?

Often this niggling feeling sits in the pit of your stomach. The discomfort we feel is alerting us to attend to a conversation that needs to be had. Ideally, we listen to that feeling rather than avoiding it. When we listen, we have an internal dialogue with ourselves. Our internal wisdom is there to guide us and remind us of our truth. If we turn our awareness to it and listen, it will remind us of what truly matters.

Mindfulness and Our Truth

As you become more mindful, you become increasingly aware of the stories you tell yourself that keep you small. You will also come to know your truth –those things that truly matter to you or that comprise who you really are. The more you let go of those stories and focus on your truth, the happier, more successful you will be.

For instance, during my first marriage, I told myself that I must not be doing a good enough job as a wife. I thought that I needed to change. I needed to try harder and do more until… I was completely exhausted. The truth is, it didn't matter how hard I tried, because trying harder wasn't the real issue. The issue was avoidance of a difficult conversation.

I needed to say out loud what I was feeling and thinking. I didn't, because I was afraid that speaking my mind would negatively impact myself and my family. So I stayed quiet for far too long. I didn't know who to turn to.

Eventually I did have the difficult conversation, and after several years of reflection (and lots of therapy) my marriage ended. During those years, the stories I told myself replayed in my head: "Divorce isn't an acceptable path. You can't break up the family. What will happen to the children? How will they cope? What if I can't cope? What will my friends, parents, relatives say? Will they understand?"

I survived, as many women and men do; however, the cost was high. There was so much unnecessary tension and so many hours wasted arguing with myself, rather than honouring my truth. The impact of this stress and anxiety was felt by the whole family.

The bottom line is, it didn't have to be that way. It's important to honour our values, even when it means facing the difficult conversation. Acknowledging and upholding our values makes us who we are. It's how we live and model happy, productive lives.

Which Wolf Do You Feed?

In the end, we have a choice. As the following legend illustrates, we can tell ourselves stories that keep us silent and afraid, or we can listen for our truth and learn how to speak it.

An old Cherokee was teaching his grandson about life. "A fight is going on inside me," he said to the boy. "It is a terrible fight and it is between two wolves One is evil: He is anger, envy, sorrow, regret, greed, arrogance, self-pity, guilt, resentment, inferiority, lies, false pride, superiority, and ego.

The other is good: He is joy, peace, love, hope, serenity, humility, kindness, benevolence, empathy, generosity, truth, compassion, and faith. The same fight is going on inside you – and inside every other person, too."

The grandson thought about it for a minute, and then asked his grandfather, "Which wolf will win?"

The old Cherokee simply replied, "The one you feed." (first people.us)

Take a moment to apply this legend to your own life.

Reflection

My bad wolf tells me: ____

____

____

____

My good wolf tells me:______________________________

____

____

____

Which wolf do you feed more often? ____________________

Can you recall a time when you needed to speak your truth but didn't? Did you struggle internally until the issue became magnified that it negatively affected your life? _________________________

What happened as a result of remaining silent? ______________

____

____

____

Did you eventually summon up the courage to have a conversation and speak your truth? If so, what was the tipping point that finally caused you to speak your mind? _________________________

____

____

____

What did you learn from that experience? ________________

____

____

____

____

Mindfulness and Your Leadership Presence

As you become mindful, you gain clarity about who you are and what you want. This enhances your leadership presence. You become someone who inspires others. But when some aspect of your life or pursuit you are engaged in is out of alignment with your core values, your presence is diminished. For instance, if your career is stagnant and your role isn't fulfilling, or if you're in an unhealthy relationship causing you sleepless nights, not only are you putting your health at risk, but you are also not honouring your values. You may be holding back out of fear that speaking up will cause conflict and people won't like you. You may worry that if you speak up you will be seen as aggressive or as a threat this can be especially true for women. The truth is the outcome of speaking up is freeing, and being true to who you are is worth it.

Facing the truth is hard. And while keeping your head in the sand may feel easier, over time it erodes our spirit. We may show up to others as distracted, withdrawn, curt, lacking energy, or insincere. All of this can impact our leadership presence. People notice when we are less engaged, and that can diminish their trust in us.

The more we try to avoid difficult situations, the louder our internal voices become until finally something shifts. Making mindfulness a daily practice starts with just a few minutes a day. Tap into your internal wisdom, listen deeply, and follow your hunch when something feels off. Not only does mindfulness practise help us lead and deal with conflict more effectively, it also centres us and calms our mind, body, and spirit.

I am not stressing the idea of establishing a mindfulness practice because I'm claiming to be a mindfulness expert; I am simply sharing what I've learned and ways that I incorporate mindfulness into my everyday life. Here's why: meditation and the practice of getting quiet and listening inward is a tool that helps you to develop full presence one moment at a time.

Mindfulness Practice

I led you through an introductory meditation in chapter 3. Are you ready to give mindfulness meditation another try?

Take 2 minutes right now. Find a quiet place to sit. Set a timer and close your eyes. Breathe calmly in and out. Relax your body and try to focus on your breath. Continue breathing, in and out. Notice when you get distracted. Each time your mind wanders, bring yourself back to your breath. When your timer goes off, open your eyes.

How did it go?____

____

____

What did you notice? ____________________________________

If you stayed with the exercise until your timer went off, good work! If not, that's okay. The goal is not about perfection. This is an exercise that develops over time, gradually reducing stress and increasing presence.

This is a very basic mindfulness meditation exercise. If you are interested in learning more and enhancing your practice, I encourage you to check out Jon Kabat-Zinn's *Mindfulness for Beginners (youtube.com).*

Bring a Powerful Presence to Any Conversation

Earlier in this chapter, we learned that to be fully present with another person we must first be present with ourselves. Mindfulness is one way to accomplish this. Another is to learn how to bring our attention back to the present moment if distracted during a conversation. For instance, have you ever been in a conversation where the other person was sharing his or her thoughts, and your mind shifted from listening to forming opinions and judgments? You may have felt the urge to jump in and tell the person what to do or how to do it (your way). Perhaps you started making assumptions that weren't based on facts or truth. You're not alone, of course. Our automatic instinct is to jump in and be the "problem-solver" is a common challenge. But it distracts us from truly listening and being in the moment.

The ability to notice when you want to jump in, and then quiet your mind and bring yourself back to the present moment, takes effort, focus, and *skill.* That skill is something you can practise and improve. Here are a few tips to help you bring a powerful presence to any conversation:

1. During your next conversation, pay attention to your desire or impulse to jump in and solve a problem. Rather than act on those thoughts, bring your awareness to them. Just take note of your thoughts.

2. If you are forming any negative feelings or judgments, take a deep breath in and release. Realize that these are only thoughts. Let them flow by.

3. Refocus on your conversation.

4. LISTEN.

As you improve your ability to stay present in the conversation, keep in mind that not every thought is there to distract you. Sometimes you may have a hunch or sense something important during a conversation. When your intuition comes into play, pay attention to it. So how do you distinguish when it's your intuition and not just another impulsive reaction or distracting thoughts? Intuition is a gentle nudge, a niggling feeling or thought that comes to you from deep within. It flows naturally from your internal wisdom, a tool we are all equipped with. As with any great muscle, intuition is strengthened with exercise. Over time you will become more confident as you learn to trust it and allow your intuition to guide your conversation.

Getting in the Zone

When you learn to quiet the noise in your head and bring a powerful presence to your conversations, you bring your *whole self*, which serves others and has more impact. It is with these kinds of conversations, when you are *in the zone*, that profound change happens.

When you are *in the zone*, nothing else matters except the conversation you are having *right here, right now*. There is no agenda aside from the other person's. There is no judgment. Talking about feelings and what's really going on can make a person feel vulnerable. Your presence makes it safe. When you are present like this for another person, they can speak from their core and dig into the issues that have held them back: things they may have never shared with anyone else before.

As they speak, remain open and curious. Keep your assumptions and opinions in check. Listen intently with a keen interest in their unique perspective. There is an aliveness when you stay in the moment; you're excited to dive into a world that is different from your own. Your senses are heightened: it's as though you're dancing in the moment.

At the same time, when you're listening deeply (which, again, means observing tone, body language, and emotions, and listening for what's not being said), you can hear the true meaning behind what is being said. You can get to the root of what's really going on. When we are focused and attuned to one another, our connection is deeper. It's as though two hearts beat as one.

This is called *Powerful Presence.*

When you experience this kind of conversation, the possibility of deep connection in the moment transforms us, one conversation at a time.

People Remember How You Made Them Feel

Clients have told me, "You make me feel like I'm the most important person on earth!" This is how it feels to be on the receiving end of presence. Your presence lets the other person know that you have their back and you're on their side. You want to know what their opportunities and challenges are, and you want to help them reach their potential.

When your team feels your authenticity, presence, and trust, they will jump through hoops to meet the goals the team has set. When they feel valued and supported, and you hold them as resourceful and capable of doing great work, they step up their game. *Believing* in your team, seeing their potential, and coaching them around their strengths supports them to move beyond the status quo toward becoming extraordinary.

Think about it. Imagine that someone you respect and trust implicitly has your back, regardless of how ambitious or far-fetched you may feel your goals are. Imagine that person sees your value, your unique gifts and capability. What would that *feel* like? Like you could conquer the world? Achieve anything you set your mind to? You betcha! Your presence can empower others to feel that way too.

Living in Your Strengths

Let's shift gears here to focus on your strengths and how they contribute to your unique presence.

We are not all motivated by the same things, and the lens through which we view the world isn't the only one. If several of us sitting around a table were asked to solve a problem, each of us would tackle it in our own way, using our unique perceptions, beliefs, values, experiences, and strengths.

As I've explained in previous chapters, you cannot lead others until you can lead yourself. Part of leading yourself is knowing what motivates *you.* For example, you may love **developing people's potential**, conducting research to help others achieve **success** or facing **new challenges**. Maybe you thrive on **leading** or **building relationships** that **help others** be successful. Perhaps one of these bolded words describes your motivating factor, an ability that comes easily to you.

If you're not tuning into your motivation, using your strengths, and expressing your values, you will feel out of sync. For example, if you asked me to do research and look at data all day long, or draw up elaborate processes and procedures, my energy would be depleted, and I'd feel unfulfilled. Although those tasks are necessary, and I appreciate their importance and value those strengths, they're not where I love to play. This is also why hiring the right people with motivations that match their role, and your vision and values, is key.

The truth is, it's hard to *show up* authentically when we aren't tapping into our own internal motivations.

Reflection

Have you ever had a job you didn't like? How did it feel? ______________

____

____

____

Do you remember the internal conflict you felt as you struggled to do the work? I've been there, and it's not fun. Maybe you feel that way about your current role. The way to avoid repeating that experience is to get very clear on what does motivate you, so that you begin to recognize the best roles that tap into your unique abilities and enable you to shine.

So, what motivates you? Are you clear on what that is?

An easy way to gain self-awareness of your values and motivations is to simply pay attention to what you gravitate towards what inspires you, and what you're passionate about. You may already know, or perhaps your work from chapter 3 helped you figure that out.

To help you dig deeper, complete the exercise below. Make a list of 20 strengths (things you're good at, passionate about) and skills that come naturally to you. Then, beside each strength, write down why it's important to you and how it makes you feel. If you can't think of 20 now, come back to this exercise as they come to you.

Here's an example:

Strength – Developing people.

It's important to me because: *it energizes me to see people's eyes light up when they talk about their goals, experience breakthroughs, and achieve things that once felt impossible to them. I love that I get to play with so many amazing, talented, intelligent people and help them live happier, more fulfilled lives.*

It excites me because: *I get to work in my passion everyday, through which I make the world a better place.*

1. Strength ______________________________

It's important to me because ______________________________

____

____

____

It excites me because ______________________________

____

____

____

2. Strength______________________________

It's important to me because ______________________________

____

____

____

It excites me because ______________________________

____

____

____

____

3. Strength_______________________________________

It's important to me because ___________________________

____

____

It excites me because ______________________________

____

____

4. Strength_______________________________________

It's important to me because ___________________________

____

____

It excites me because ______________________________

____

____

5. Strength _______________________________________

It's important to me because ___________________________

____

____

It excites me because ______________________________

____

____

6. Strength_______________________________________

It's important to me because ___________________________

____

____

____

It excites me because ______________________________

____

____

7. Strength_______________________________________

It's important to me because ____

____

____

____

It excites me because ____

____

____

____

8. Strength____

It's important to me because ____

____

____

____

It excites me because ____

____

____

____

9. Strength ____

It's important to me because ____

____

____

____

It excites me because ____

____

____

____

10. Strength ____

It's important to me because ____

____

____

It excites me because ____

____

11. Strength ____

It's important to me because ___________________________
____
____

It excites me because _________________________________
____
____

12. Strength ____

It's important to me because ___________________________
____
____

It excites me because _________________________________
____
____

13. Strength ____

It's important to me because ___________________________
____
____

It excites me because _________________________________
____
____

14. Strength ____

It's important to me because ___________________________
____
____

It excites me because _________________________________
____
____

15. Strength ____

It's important to me because ___________________________

It excites me because

16. Strength

It's important to me because

It excites me because

17. Strength

It's important to me because

It excites me because

18. Strength

It's important to me because

It excites me because

19. Strength

It's important to me because

It excites me because ______________________________________

____

____

20. Strength ____

It's important to me because _________________________________

____

____

It excites me because ______________________________________

____

____

Good work on creating a list of your strengths and articulating their importance!

How do your values link to your strengths? ____________________

____

____

What surprised you? ____

____

____

In your current role, do you have the opportunity to tap into your strengths frequently? It's important to step back from time to time to check how aligned your career/work/life choices are with your values and strengths. If they're not, what would help you become more aligned? Sometimes we may feel off-kilter and not understand why, especially when we are going through change at work and using fewer and fewer of our strengths. Of course, the same holds true for those you coach.

If you would like to take this work further, there are numerous brilliant self-assessments and emotional intelligence tools designed to help you learn more about your strengths and values One of my favourites is the Strengths Deployment Inventory (SDI), which is a relationship awareness tool developed by Elias Porter, Ph.D., to help you understand what motivates you and your team. I use it to help my clients become aware of their motivations, as well as to inform myself of their values, strengths, and motivating forces. This helps me be a more effective coach.

Becoming crystal clear on what motivates you (and your team) allows you to harness your strengths and articulate them to your clients, prospects, team, or organization so they understand the value you bring. Aligning your values with your passion is essential in helping you make better choices so that you can live your most authentic life. This ties in with *presence*. This deeper understanding of your strengths, and motivations helps to create a powerful leadership presence that others will want to emulate.

The External Dimension of Presence

The old adage is true: You only get one chance to make a good first impression. As I said at the start of this chapter, a powerful leadership presence begins on the inside. However, the external dimension–your image–is an integral part of a powerful presence and success in business. It's just as influential as your internal awareness–the way you interact and listen to others.

First, let me clarify: What you wear and how you look doesn't have anything to do with your intelligence or competence. However, since you only get that one chance, why not boost your odds by incorporating the tips in this section to be more certain that you are putting your best foot forward? After all, you are your brand. (This also holds true for everything that surrounds you, such as your website, marketing, and communications.)

I'm aware that this topic may feel a little frivolous, and may trigger some beliefs or perceptions, so let me speak to this directly. Many women and men simply don't have a natural ability to know what colours work best for their skin tone, what the optimal clothing is for their body type, or what fashion personality suits them the best. If we don't have that knowledge, we may lack confidence, or it may simply be a blind spot. While the information in this section doesn't replace the personal attention of an image consultant, my hope is that the practical tips below will put you on the path to greater mastery of how you feel in your clothing, and greater confidence as you present your best self.

Enhancing your appearance is not about creating a façade; it's about putting the best version of you out there and ensuring your first impression is powerful and impactful.

When we take care of our appearance, and like what and who we see in the mirror, we feel a greater sense of joy and confidence that anything is possible. In that moment, we can conquer the world.

How to Enhance Your External Presence

As you know, I invested more than a decade gaining knowledge and expertise in image consulting. I know from experience that a picture paints a thousand words, and like it or not, we all have biases and judge others by their appearance. Your hair, clothing style, fit and colour, cosmetics, and accessories all connect to how you physically *show up*. They communicate confidence or lack thereof. You've heard the expression "When you look good, you feel good"? It's true. There's just no way around it. The norms may have relaxed a bit over recent years, but it's proven that women and men in business are far more successful if they present themselves in a professional manner.

I'm not suggesting you go out today and max your credit cards on a new wardrobe. However, if you need further assistance in this area, investing some time and money to learn what style of clothing suits your body type, and what colours make you feel alive and work best with your skin tone (for both your wardrobe and cosmetics) can pay off time and time again. Discovering these key elements will remove anxiety, time, and costly shopping errors by taking the guesswork out of your shopping experience. You will feel knowledgeable and confident in your purchases and in your appearance.

What constitutes dressing in a "professional manner" varies depending on the type of work you do, your business environment, who you're meeting with and, often, your gender. The key is to have a sense of how to dress for the occasion. In addition to your appearance, body language is a big part of embodying a powerful presence. Maintaining eye contact, having a firm (not crushing or limp) handshake, an engaging smile, and a warm hello will help to make a great first impression.

It remains true that women have more options when it comes to style, but it's important to understand we all have our own unique style that we like to express. It is based on many things, including your physical characteristics, personal preference, and the environment that you live and work in. I decided to have some fun with the four basic fashion personalities that typically apply to women–Natural, Romantic, Classic, and Dramatic–and open them up to everyone.

No fashion personality is better than the other, and typically you gravitate toward two. There are several fashion personality tests online that can help you identify yours. Knowing which two you most resonate with can help you portray your best self, because your outfit will be a natural fit with who you are. By sharpening your style up a bit for business occasions, you will also look good and feel great. Your image needs to pull together from head to toe, meaning hair style (grooming), makeup, accessories, and outfit, right down to shoes, are important aspects of putting your best image forward.

Naturals love a casual look, with comfort being the number-one priority. They prefer relaxed clothing such as jeans, loose trousers, maxi skirts, and slouchy knits. Since they like their clothing and fabrics to feel super-comfortable, ***Natural*** types prefer not to dress up. If worn at all, cosmetics and jewellery tend to be a kept to a minimum, and flat shoes are the norm.

There is nothing wrong with a casual look. If, however, you don't want to fall under the radar at work, find a way to add a little pizzazz to your look and/or take it up a notch to "business casual." Keep it natural but pulled together, so others see you as a professional and you get noticed for promotions and attract new clients. For example, women might add shoes with a small heel, a semi-tailored pant (there are so many comfortable styles available today), and a soft, textured tweed jacket to create a more professional look. Apply a little mascara, a muted lip colour, a little blush to add definition, and don't be afraid to add a little detail such as earrings and a scarf for a pop of colour! All of these will go far to ensure you get noticed while remaining true to your Natural fashion personality.

Men: Your best image is clean-shaven, your hair and beard trimmed. Trade in your tennis shoes and jeans for a pair of casual leather dress shoes, a crisp white shirt, casual pant, and a sport jacket. Again, keep your work environment in mind. How do your male counterparts or supervisors dress? In some cases, you may need to lead the way. Aim for a natural look within this target zone.

A good rule of thumb for everyone is to dress a notch above the audience you are presenting to. If your clients are in jeans, wear business casual. If they're in suits, choose something with pizzazz, especially if you're speaking on stage. Men, if your male supervisor, VP, or CEO wears a suit or dressy trousers, and you aspire to move up to their level, dress the part!

Classics are all about beautifully elegant yet simple pieces: crisp shirts, tailored jackets, and trousers. Solid colours versus patterns. Pearls and timeless jewellery. Feminine Classics view cosmetics as an accessory just like jewellery and are drawn to muted tones and classic lip colour. If you're a ***Classic*** type you may have a lot of neutral colours in your closet (black, navy, and a little white). Your style aligns well with traditional business attire for men and women, and you're very comfortable wearing a suit. You may feel challenged or a bit overdressed in more casual work environments, so find out the dress code before your meeting. Wear a pop of colour in a scarf or tie, and women can add a one-of-a-kind piece of chunky jewellery to add a little pizzazz.

The ***Romantic*** fashion personality is a traditional feminine look. ***Romantics*** gravitate toward ruffles, lace, floral prints, flowy pants, blouses and skirts, pearls and antique-style jewellery. Cosmetics tend toward soft pinks and blush-coloured pastels. Again, this style is soft and feminine; however, it can sometimes show up as too "girlie" and potentially weak, putting you at risk of being overlooked for a promotion or not taken seriously in the business world.

Both men and women can tweak this style to find a nice balance of soft and feminine yet professional. If you are attending a business meeting, add a little oomph to your look by wearing less ruffles or lace and adding a tailored jacket to give your style an understated confidence.

Dramatics love trendsetting styles that stand out. You can spot them a mile away. While Naturals feel that less is more, ***Dramatics*** are all about more is better. They love vibrant colours and unique statement pieces. High heels and chunky jewellery complete their look. Cosmetics are played up with bold colour. Dramatic men will sport flashy ties, jackets or shirts, funky socks, or gender-bending clothing.

The dramatic look can be powerful and persuasive, but if yours is a dramatic style, be careful not to overdo it. If you arrive at a daytime meeting dressed for an evening out, you will look out of place. Tone it down a little for a daytime meeting and save the brighter pops of colour (cosmetics, jewellery, etc.) for the evening. Too many accessories tend to look overdone. One statement piece is ideal.

Please, please, please, one ring per hand. Find a nice ring to feature. Too many rings on your fingers are distracting and will cheapen your look and come across as though you couldn't decide so you wore all of them!

Which two fashion personalities do you resonate with? ____________

____

____

____

I am a ***Natural-Classic***, which means I love to wear timeless clothing with elegance and grace. Lots of solid colours fill my closet (is there such a thing as too much black?). I prefer classic and comfort over trendy. After work you'll find me in a pair of jeans with a casual loose top and a pair of boots or flats. On the weekends I (almost) never leave home without my lipstick and earrings!

Choosing clothing and accessories that align with both of your fashion personalities is fun and adds dimension to your wardrobe. Sticking with your two fashion personalities creates a wardrobe that is easy to coordinate from head to toe. You know those items in your closet that just don't "feel right" and never leave the hanger? They may have looked nice in the store, or on your friend, but the style probably *just isn't you.* By understanding your fashion personality, you can more easily resist the urge to buy, for instance, a floral top, if you know you are a ***Classic***.

Know Your Audience

Regardless of your style, know yourself, know your audience, and dress accordingly. There is a big difference between what you wear to a business meeting versus speaking on stage to hundreds of people.

Always be authentic. Ask yourself, *Who am I meeting with? What's the dress code for the meeting/convention? What image do I want to portray? What impression do I want to leave?* Then listen for cues from your intuition.

What does your gut tell you? Taking time to check in with yourself will help you set your intention for how you want to show up, preserve authentically for each situation so you show up confidently.

Be mindful of your appearance, even if you're just popping out to the store, because you never know who you might bump into. It only takes 2 minutes to make yourself presentable before you walk out the door. Being prepared and mindful of important meetings that day can make or break your success.

A few years ago, I was connecting with potential business partners and met a colleague who was selling a product that interested me. When we met, I was shocked to see that she looked as though she'd just finished cleaning her house, rather than prepared for a business meeting with a potential prospect. Before I even heard the first word from her mouth, I was thinking, "Hmm, I won't be working with her." I didn't. I made the decision within the first few seconds of meeting her. Was this fair? Maybe not. But the fact is, this is how our brain works, assessing in the moment. How could I trust that she would show up professionally with clients? To me, she didn't show up professionally, and I knew this didn't align with my brand.

On another occasion, I was on a plane travelling back from meetings when the person seated beside me began sharing information about her business with me. She showed me all of the products in her catalogue, but I was distracted by her haphazard appearance and the sweat pants she was wearing. I give her credit for having the courage to attempt the sale, but that wasn't enough to earn it. If she had spent a little time on her appearance, she would have increased her odds. Again, this may sound judgmental, but we all make similar assessments. My amygdala told me something felt off, that it wasn't the right fit.

This can work both ways, of course. A colleague of mine landed a big client while test-driving an automobile. You can bet she thanked her intuition for the nudge to change out of her jeans into business casual and throw her snazzy new business cards into her purse before heading out the door. The bottom line is, you never know who you are going to meet. When you're in business, always be on the lookout for new clients and prospects and remember, ABP! Always Be Prepared, internally and externally.

Presenting Your Best Image - Points to Consider

When answering the following questions, be honest. Get feedback from a close friend or family member, and don't beat yourself up. You are where you are, and I want to encourage you to refresh your look every so often. When done well, it will put a bounce in your step. Remember your image is YOUR brand.

What does your image say about you? ______________________________

____

____

____

What part of putting yourself together comes easily to you? What is challenging?____

____

____

When did you last update your wardrobe/hairstyle/cosmetics/glasses?

____

____

____

How does your wardrobe align (or not) with your career/business/life? What needs your attention? ________________________________

____

____

____

When was the last time you went through your closet and purged or donated clothing that no longer works for you? _________________

____

____

____

Are you ready for a new look? What image updates are you ready for?

____

____

____

____

Presenting a professional image can be a daunting task, I get it. By taking it step by step, you will start to notice your confidence growing. I have experienced firsthand the effects of improving one's personal image. It's also part of self-care, so don't wait another day to get out there and have fun with it. To get yourself started, find images and words that resonate with you to inspire your personal brand (part of your leadership presence). For example, images and words that resonate with me are beautiful Zen beaches and inspiring messages. This speaks to my calm leadership presence that inspires others.

Bringing It All Together

Let's take what you've learned about the internal and external dimensions of presence further.

Reflection

What does leadership presence mean to you?____________________

____

____

What is the experience that you want people to have when they interact with you? ____

____

____

Sometimes how we think we *show up*, or how we are *being*, is different from what we are putting out there and how others experience us. Asking for candid feedback from those you trust can help you determine if your unique presence is truly aligned with the experience you most want to create.

"What counts in life is not the mere fact that we have lived. It is what difference we have made to the lives of others that will determine the significance of the life we have led."

– Nelson Mandela

Chapter 7

What Will Be Your Legacy?

Several years ago while waiting for a flight, I was drawn to a sign across the room that read, "Legacy Leaders aren't born, they are nurtured." At the time I wondered what that meant. I have come to understand that leaders aren't born leaders. They are nurtured by great mentors or coaches who help them to grow and reach beyond what they can imagine for themselves. Many coaches and mentors have pushed my limits. They played a significant role in my development over the years, and I learned so much about myself in the process. I strive to do the same for those I coach. Acknowledging our mentors helps us remember how we got to where we are and reminds us of our responsibility as leaders. Growing and nurturing others becomes part of our legacy.

Who helped shape the person you are today? ____________________

____

____

____

Johann Wolfgang von Goethe once said, "If we treat people as they are, they will remain as they are. If we treat them as they ought to be, they will become what they ought to be."

Extraordinary leaders understand how to treat people as they ought to be. They do this by acquiring the knowledge, tools ,and skills needed to help others grow beyond their current state, and then by having conversations that take their clients into the future. They encourage their clients to cultivate their own unique brilliance and tap into their inner wisdom to know for themselves what needs to shift as they move toward their ideal future state. Extraordinary leaders understand the significance of not only creating a future vision, but, more importantly, committing it to paper and holding true to that vision every day with consistent effort. They know that their own true success lies in developing others who will leave their companies, communities, and world a better place. Extraordinary leaders are also legacy builders. As coaches, it is our responsibility to develop the leaders of tomorrow. Ultimately, they will be responsible for their own actions, and we are simply the conduit to help them realize their potential. Those leaders are part of the legacy that we leave behind.

Leadership Mastery Self-Assessment

In the last chapter we talked about the internal and external elements of developing a powerful leadership presence. You also know by now that it is possible to become extraordinary. In fact, you have already done a lot of that work throughout these chapters (and in the years before your hands even touched this book) and have set a solid foundation to live with intentional and greater fulfillment. Let's take some time now to assess how far you've come.

Read the statements beside each competency and determine where you are on a scale of 1to10. Place your number beside each competency.

1: The statement doesn't accurately describe you You rarely model this competency.

5: You sometimes model this competency, but you know this is an area you could develop further.

10: The statement accurately describes you, and you consistently model this competency for yourself and others.

Confidence: You have an unwavering belief in yourself and are not swayed by the negative opinions of others. You trust in your own unique ability, and you achieve whatever you set your mind to. Your confidence shines through whether you're engaging one-on-one or in front of a large group.

☐	☐	☐	☐	☐	☐	☐	☐	☐	☐
1	2	3	4	5	6	7	8	9	10

Clarity: You have a clear vision for your future and articulate that vision concisely. You have the ability to create clarity for others around complex situations, which helps them move forward in a positive way.

☐	☐	☐	☐	☐	☐	☐	☐	☐	☐
1	2	3	4	5	6	7	8	9	10

Mindfulness: You have a deep knowledge of self and a highly tuned awareness of your internal and external being. You are grounded and feel centred most of the time. You observe your thoughts, feelings, attitudes, and desires non-judgmentally, rather than identifying with them and staying "stuck." You have a good grasp of the mind/body/spirit connection.

☐	☐	☐	☐	☐	☐	☐	☐	☐	☐
1	2	3	4	5	6	7	8	9	10

Trust: You are sincere and respectful. You are open and allow others into your life, providing a safe place for them to be. You trust your decisions as well as the decisions of others. They know what the right path is for them.

☐	☐	☐	☐	☐	☐	☐	☐	☐	☐
1	2	3	4	5	6	7	8	9	10

Authenticity: You communicate transparently and are able to connect naturally with others. You're genuine and true to who you are, not what you think others expect of you. You provide genuine, meaningful feedback to help others grow.

☐	☐	☐	☐	☐	☐	☐	☐	☐	☐
1	2	3	4	5	6	7	8	9	10

Presence: You convey a professional presence that leaves a lasting impression. Your presence communicates your unique style, brand, and the company you represent. You bring a powerful presence to conversations that demand your best.

☐	☐	☐	☐	☐	☐	☐	☐	☐	☐
1	2	3	4	5	6	7	8	9	10

Courage: You go after what you want, even in the face of fear, resistance, or uncertainty. You speak the truth and put courageous conversations on the table, even when everyone else seems to turn a blind eye. You challenge the status quo when necessary. You stretch yourself, and are a lifelong learner.

☐	☐	☐	☐	☐	☐	☐	☐	☐	☐
1	2	3	4	5	6	7	8	9	10

Integrity: Your decisions are aligned with your strengths, goals, and values. You consistently demonstrate honesty, ethics, and boundaries, communicating them clearly to the people in your life.

☐ 1 ☐ 2 ☐ 3 ☐ 4 ☐ 5 ☐ 6 ☐ 7 ☐ 8 ☐ 9 ☐ 10

Intuition: You are highly intuitive and trust your internal wisdom to guide you in your life, and in your coaching conversations. Your strong sensing ability enables you to trust your instincts and move forward without needing the validation of rational thought or conscious reasoning.

☐ 1 ☐ 2 ☐ 3 ☐ 4 ☐ 5 ☐ 6 ☐ 7 ☐ 8 ☐ 9 ☐ 10

Listening/Communication: You have the ability to listen beyond spoken words, which allows you to zero in on what is truly being said. You communicate effectively, ask powerful questions, are able to see things objectively, and do not get caught in other people's stories.

☐ 1 ☐ 2 ☐ 3 ☐ 4 ☐ 5 ☐ 6 ☐ 7 ☐ 8 ☐ 9 ☐ 10

Inspiration: You have faith in those you support and hold their vision, even when they've lost sight of it. You inspire people to action by helping them overcome obstacles, celebrating their successes, and reminding them who they are and what they're capable of.

☐ 1 ☐ 2 ☐ 3 ☐ 4 ☐ 5 ☐ 6 ☐ 7 ☐ 8 ☐ 9 ☐ 10

Accountability: You hold yourself and others accountable to the goals set. You do what you say you will do. People can count on you to follow through on your commitments.

☐ 1 ☐ 2 ☐ 3 ☐ 4 ☐ 5 ☐ 6 ☐ 7 ☐ 8 ☐ 9 ☐ 10

Add up your score: ________

If your score is 110 or higher, congratulations! You are doing extraordinary work and leaving a legacy! Continue to pay attention to these competencies and find new ways to learn and grow.

If your score is between 75 and 109, you're becoming an extraordinary leader who models the way for others. Continue to put yourself in the learner seat, keep stretching, and review these competencies regularly to check in and monitor your progress.

If your score is below 75, this is an opportunity to further develop these competencies, that will support you now and in the future. You are where you are. Each of us moves along a continuum of personal growth, and learning is a constant evolution of practice and refinement. Be patient and kind to yourself.

The journey toward being an extraordinary leader is a journey toward personal mastery, not a destination that we arrive at and then quit. Life is a learning lab; the discovery is continuous. You know what you know, and you don't know what you don't know, and that's okay. No matter what stage you're at, a little refining goes a long way and can make a big difference in how you lead yourself and others. Even if you scored above 110, there are always opportunities for growth.

Reflection

What do your results tell you? ______________________________

____

____

____

____

____

____

Which competencies come easily to you? ______________________

____

____

____

Identify three areas you most want to work on:

1.____
2.____
3.____

Your Road Map to Success

You've learned about the basics of coaching, why it's effective, how to take these skills into your everyday conversations, and the value of developing a coaching culture. You've increased your awareness about the power of presence through mindfulness and openness to your internal wisdom. You are busting through limiting beliefs and are about to embark on big change. By identifying your big vision, overcoming obstacles and creating action steps, you are designing your Road Map to Success.

As you build your road map, here are four action steps to include:

1. Cement what you've learned about being an extraordinary leader by revisiting the exercises in this book. Start to implement what you've learned on a daily basis.

2. Revisit your big, bold, courageous vision from chapter 3. Create a solid plan. Break down your BIG goal into bite sizes (e.g., monthly goals, and weekly and daily actions). What do you need to do each day to stay inspired and on track. (Vision boards are a great tool to help you keep your goal front and centre.)

3. Implement your plan and find an accountability partner, someone who will hold your feet to the fire. Identify gaps in your knowledge and get support where needed.

4. Visualize its completion. One day, while working on this manuscript, my daughter asked, "Why are you sighing?"

I replied, "Because I'm on the home stretch of my book. I'm really starting to feel the power of its completion and it feels really good!" At that moment I was visualizing the night of my book launch and celebration. I could see the space and the people in the room. It was all abuzz! As I imagined the launch, I felt immense gratitude for what felt like a massive push through fear and resistance as I was nearing the finish line.

When you are trying to achieve something you have never done before, visualizing the experience of reaching your goal is a very powerful tool to help you bring your vision to reality. Remember, what you focus on grows. Give yourself permission to go there–even if you don't know the how yet. Visualize what it will feel like in that moment when you've completed the project or attained the goal that's been in your heart for a long time. For me, it was finally holding this book in my hands.

Reflection

What about you?

How will you celebrate? ______________________________

____

____

____

Who will be there? ______________________________

____

____

____

What will that experience feel like? ______________________________

____

____

____

Where are you celebrating? What does the room look like? Paint a clear picture in your mind and revisit it along the way as you bring your goal to fruition. ______________________________

____

____

____

If you are trying to attain a goal that's new, expect some challenges and bumps in the road. Celebrate the small wins along the way.

Congratulations! You have come this far, and you've mapped out a plan for what you really want.

You have what you need within to guide you. You simply need to listen. If you're not doing what you love, are ready for something bigger, and know you need support to help you reach your goals, I invite you to take the next step with me. I'd love to help you move forward in a big way so that you can live and lead with passion, intention, and unwavering commitment. Read on to find out how!

"Take the first step in faith. You don't have to see the whole staircase, just take the first step."

– Martin Luther King Jr.

If you made it here, my sense is you're ready for more... Excellent!

I'm excited you are here. If you are feeling inspired and want to take your learning deeper, you will love what's next!

"After extensive research on a plethora of coaching courses, I decided on **The Coach Approach System™** as my coach training resource. It has impacted me both personally and professionally. I have confidence, composure and clarity as a coach. I'm applying the skills during coaching conversations with my colleagues and plan to use this approach with my clients. Now I'm on top of life, life is no longer on top of me!"

Adaora Ayoade, ACC
CEO of EZ37 Solutions Ltd.

Several years ago, I saw a gap and knew I could help managers and leaders become more effective by developing coaching skills to empower their teams.

My goal was twofold:

1. To create flexible coaching programs that transform the way leaders work, live, and lead around the globe.
2. To help thousands of coaches make more money, have more impact, and turn their dreams into reality by doing work they love.

My result **The Coach Approach System™** accredited coach training programs for all leaders and coaches.

Bring coaching skills into your organization to **unleash leadership potential!**

The Coach Approach System™ Level 1: Leadership and Coaching Foundations for All Leaders.

This coach training program is designed to help you develop the most relevant leadership skills and become more effective in your role. These foundational skills will help you feel less stressed and more productive, and experience greater results in your work! This highly interactive training is delivered both live and online, and is perfect for coaches, aspiring coaches, managers, and leaders wanting to have more impact in their work and in the lives of others. **The Coach Approach System™ Level 1** will help you get clear about your goals, break through limiting beliefs, and shift your mindset to help you grow beyond your current state. This experiential training includes coaching skills practise and feedback grounded in the ICF core competencies to help you become a better listener and extraordinary coach. Walk away with skills, tools, and a proven method for successful coaching conversations, based on science and the latest research, linked to increase ROI.

To learn more about **The Coach Approach System™**, please visit us at www.pamgriffithscoaching.com.

"I was fortunate to have the opportunity to participate in **The Coach Approach System™** with Pam and her team. While I have been coaching for many years, I can tell you that Pam and her team took the group on a very different experiential journey that was invaluable both professionally and personally. Experiencing mindfulness, embracing authenticity and vulnerability are all key elements to build a solid coaching foundation.

Pam guides participants through this process with ease and significant expertise. For anyone who thinks they understand coaching, Pam and the team offer a truly transformational experience, enabling both the development and enhancement of capabilities so critical to a coach's success."

Kim Kernohan, Director, HR Business Partners & Talent Acquisition, Meridian™

Do you want to build high-performing teams and lead culture change in your organization?

The Coach Approach System™ Level II: Leading Culture Change and High Performing Teams.

Deepen your coaching skills and coach your team to new heights. This experiential coach training program introduces the key concepts of what motivates yourself and others so you can effectively engage your team and increase performance. You'll discover the ROI of coaching teams and walk away with the foundational framework and a plan to implement a coaching culture that you can use right away within your organization or coaching practice.

To learn more about **The Coach Approach System™ Level II,** please visit us at www.pamgriffithscoaching.com.

The Coach Approach System™ is a registered trademark of PGEC.

Become a certified The Coach Approach System™ facilitator

If you have a passion for coaching and are looking for a done-for-you product to grow your business and support your clients, you can apply to become a certified facilitator of **The Coach Approach System™**. To learn more about our train-the-trainer program prerequisites and qualifications email us at info@pamgriffithscoaching.com. Our certification process is available for qualified coaches who love facilitating, developing others and want to have greater impact.*

* *Available for organizations who want to develop leaders as coaches.*

ABOUT THE AUTHOR

Pam Griffiths, CEO of Pam Griffiths Coaching, is an author and speaker, and a Professional Certified Coach (PCC) through the International Coach Federation (ICF). With more than two decades coaching high-performing leaders, Pam has gained a deep understanding of what motivates individuals and a profound intuition that helps her clients achieve extraordinary results.

In the midst of a rigorous coach training program several years ago, Pam realized that a coaching methodology is a common missing link among leaders, and a vital tool that they can use to lead self and others toward greater success. This realization led her to create the Coach Approach System™, an ICF-accredited coach training program that equips leaders and coaches to lead with authenticity and courage by providing the necessary tools and coaching methodology to lead effectively today.

After 25 years in both the corporate and entrepreneurial arena, Pam understands the level of commitment required to grow both business and people. Pam is the coaches' coach. She is committed to supporting coaches to develop sustainable businesses through her 6-Figure Business Development Program, and leads high-achieving teams, executives, and groups toward extraordinary growth by aligning their strengths, values, and goals.

Pam and her team, coach C-suite to emerging leaders around the globe. They are passionate about helping good leaders to become extraordinary. She partners with organizations that are ready for growth, want to build capability and experience unprecedented results by infusing a coach approach into their leadership. Pam has worked closely with organizations across numerous industries–from telecommunications, high-tech, automotive, and financial services to the health care, public, and not-for-profit sectors.

WORKS CITED

Arnold, Jackie. *Coaching Skills for Leaders in the Workplace: How to Motivate and Get the Best from Your Staff.* How To Books, 2013.

Coach Federation. International Coach Federation, 2018, coachfederation.org. Accessed 26 Sep. 2018.

Collins, Jim. *Good to Great.* New York: Harper-Collins. 2001

Cuddy, Amy. *Presence: Bringing Your Boldest Self to Your Biggest Challenges.* Hachette UK, 2015.

Detrixhe, John. "The Fed has a $4 trillion problem when the next recession hits." *Quartz,* 16 Jun. 2017, www.qz.com/1006806/the-us-federal-reserve-has-a-4-trillion-problem-when-the-next-recession-hits. Accessed 26 Sep. 2018.

Dickler, Jessica. "The 10 best companies to work for in America." *CNBC,* 6 Dec. 2017, www.cnbc.com/2017/12/05/the-10-best-companies-to-work-for-in-2018. Accessed 26 Sep. 2018.

Gardner, Howard. "Frames of Mind: The Idea of Multiple Intelligence." *New York, NY* (1983).

Gocmen, Dogan. *Adam Smith Problem: Reconciling Human Nature and Society in the theory of Moral.* IB Tauris, 2007.

Gordon, Evian, et al. "An" integrative neuroscience" platform: application to profiles of negativity and positivity bias." *Journal of Integrative Neuroscience* 7.03 (2008): 345–66.

"Great Place to Work Report" *Great Place to Work,* 2016, www.greatplacetowork.ca/images/article/BusinessCase_DetailedReport_Final-1-2.pdf. Accessed 26 Sep. 2018.

Hargrove, Robert. *Masterful Coaching.* San Francisco: John Wiley & Sons, 2008.

Howlett, N., Pine, K., Orakçıoğlu, I., & Fletcher, B. "The influence of clothing on first impressions: Rapid and positive responses to minor changes in male attire." *Journal of Fashion Marketing and Management: An International Journal* 17.1 (2013): 38–48.

"Jon Kabat-Zinn, PhD - Mindfulness for Beginners (Audio Excerpt)." *YouTube*, uploaded by Sounds True, 20 Oct. 2014, www.youtube.com/watch?v=NxYFxjZBqHg

Lawson, K. L., et. al. "The Impact of Telephonic Health Coaching on Health Outcomes in a High-risk Population." *Global Advances in Health and Medicine*. 2013 May; 2(3): 40–7. Accessed 24 September 2018. www.ncbi.nlm.nih.gov/pubmed/24416671.

Leiter, Michael P., and Christina Maslach. *Banishing Burnout: Six Strategies for Improving Your Relationship with Work*. John Wiley & Sons, 2005.

Long, Heather. "The New Normal: 4 Job Changes by the Time You're 32." *CNNMoney*. Cable News Network, 12 April 2016. Accessed 20 April 2017.

Marsh, Jason. "A Little Meditation Goes A Long Way." *Greater Good*, 9 Feb. 2011, greatergood.berkeley.edu/article/item/a_little_meditation_goes_a_long_way. Accessed 26 Sep. 2018.

Murphy, Nora A. "Appearing smart: The impression management of intelligence, person perception accuracy, and behavior in social interaction." *Personality and Social Psychology Bulletin* 33.3 (2007): 325–39.

NASA History. National Aeronautics and Space Administration, 2018, history.nasa.gov. Accessed 26 Sep. 2018.

Niemiec, Ryan M., and Judith Lissing. "Mindfulness-based strengths practice (MBSP) for enhancing well-being, managing problems, and boosting positive relationships." *Mindfulness in Positive Psychology: The Science of Meditation and Wellbeing* (2016): 15–36.

Olivero, Gerald, K. Denise Bane, and Richard E. Kopelman. "Executive coaching as a transfer of training tool: Effects on productivity in a public agency." *Public Personnel Management* 26.4 (1997): 461–69.

Robinson, Sir Ken. "Changing Education Paradigms." The RSA. Feb. 2010. Lecture.

Robinson, Sir Ken. "Do Schools Kill Creativity." TED. Feb. 2006. Lecture.

Rock, David, and Jeffrey Schwartz. "The Neuroscience of Leadership." *Strategy+Business* 43 (2006).

Sandberg, Sheryl. *Lean In: Women, Work, and the Will to Lead.* Random House, 2013.

Senge, Peter. *The Fifth Discipline.* New York: Random House, 1990.

"State of the Global Workplace Report" *Gallup*, 2013, www.gallup.com/services/176735/state-global-workplace.aspx.

"Steve Jobs' 2005 Stanford Commencement Address." *YouTube*, uploaded by Stanford, 7 Mar. 2008, www.youtube.com/watch?v=UF8uR6Z6KLc.

Parker-Wilkins, Vernita. "Business impact of executive coaching: demonstrating monetary value." *Industrial and Commercial Training* 38.3 (2006): 122–27. doi.org/10.1108/00197850610659373. Accessed 26 Sep. 2018.

Pink, Dan. *The Surprising Truths About What Motivates Us.* New York: Riverhead, 2009.

Prochaska, James O., and Carlo C. DiClemente. "Transtheoretical therapy: toward a more integrative model of change." *Psychotherapy: Theory, Research & Practice* 19.3 (1982): 276–88. doi: http://dx.doi.org/10.1037/h0088437. Accessed 26 Sep. 2018.

Rock, David. "SCARF: A brain-based model for collaborating with and influencing others." *NeuroLeadership Journal* 1.1 (2008): 44–52. www.epa.gov/sites/production/files/2015-09/documents/thurs_georgia_9_10_915_covello.pdf. Accessed 26 Sep. 2018.

Smith, Linda L., et al. "Integrative Health Coach Training: A Model for Shifting the Paradigm Toward Patient-centricity and Meeting New National Prevention Goals" *Global Advances in Health and Medicine.* 2013 May; 2(3): 66–74. Published online 2013 May 1. Accessed 24 September 2018.doi: 10.7453/gahmj.2013.034.

Symonds, Matt. "Executive Coaching - Another Set of Clothes for the Emperor?" *Forbes*. 21 January 2011. www.forbes.com/sites/mattsymonds/2011/01/21/executive-coaching-another-set-of-clothes-for-the-emperor/#53e5e3e0118b. Accessed 24 Sep. 2018.

Tolle, Eckart. *A New Earth: Awakening To Your Life's Purpose*. New York: Penguin, 2005.

"Two Wolves A Cherokee Legend." *First People*, http://www.firstpeople.us/FP-Html-Legends/TwoWolves-Cherokee.html. Accessed 26 Sep. 2018

Wilcox, Laura. "Emotional Intelligence is No Soft Skill." *Harvard*. www.extension.harvard.edu/professional-development/blog/emotional-intelligence-no-soft-skill. Accessed 20 Sept. 2018.

Williamson, Marianne. *A Return To Love: Reflections on the Principles of A Course in Miracles*, San Francisco: HarperCollins, 1992. p. 190

"Workplace Conflict And How Businesses Can Harness It To Thrive" *CPP Global Human Capital Report*, 2008, www.img.en25.com/Web/CPP/Conflict_report.pdf. Accessed 26 Sep. 2018

Resources: International Coach Federation coachfederation.org.